Changing neighbourhoods

Changing neighbourhoods

Lessons from the JRF Neighbourhood Programme

Marilyn Taylor, Mandy Wilson, Derrick Purdue and Pete Wilde

JOSEPH ROWNTREE
FOUNDATION

First published in Great Britain in 2007 by

The Policy Press
Fourth Floor, Beacon House
Queen's Road
Bristol BS8 1QU
UK

Tel no   +44 (0)117 331 4054
Fax no   +44 (0)117 331 4093
Email   tpp-info@bristol.ac.uk
www.policypress.org.uk

Published for the Joseph Rowntree Foundation by The Policy Press

ISBN 978 1 86134 977 4

British Library Cataloguing in Publication Data
A catalogue record for this book is available from the British Library.

Library of Congress Cataloging-in-Publication Data
A catalog record for this book has been requested.

Marilyn Taylor is Professor of Urban Governance and Regeneration at University of the West of England, Bristol. **Mandy Wilson** is a director of COGS (Communities and Organisations: Growth and Support), a research and training consultancy based in Sheffield. **Derrick Purdue** is Senior Research Fellow in the Cities Research Centre at University of the West of England, Bristol. **Pete Wilde** is a director of COGS.

The **Joseph Rowntree Foundation** has supported this project as part of its programme of research and innovative development projects, which it hopes will be of value to policy makers, practitioners and service users. The facts presented and views expressed in this report are, however, those of the authors and not necessarily those of the Foundation.

Photos: the photos taken in Broad Street, Eastfields, East Pollokshields, Norfolk Park, Pilton and St Pauls are by Kippa Matthews. All other photos are from the neighbourhoods in the Programme or from JRF networking events.

Cover: community work in St Pauls, Bristol. Neighbourhood Renewal facilitator, Lyn Sharry, shares a joke with a resident. Photo taken by Kippa Matthews.
Cover design by Qube Design Associates, Bristol
Printed in Great Britain by Latimer Trend, Plymouth

Contents

List of tables, figures and boxes

Tables

Figures

Boxes

Acknowledgements

This report owes its existence to the energies of a large number of people, first and foremost to the members of the 20 organisations who participated in the Programme and contributed actively to the evaluation – particularly through the networking meetings and their annual reviews. As Programme manager, John Low has made a particularly important contribution both to the work of the Programme and to this report, along with the five facilitators – Michael Carley, Jenny Lynn, Trish McCue, Chris Wadhams and Mel Witherden – all of whom have contributed important insights. Their comments on earlier drafts of this document have been invaluable. Special thanks, as members of the evaluation team, are due to Theresa McDonagh, who was the JRF officer responsible for the evaluation and who gave unstinting support as we negotiated an appropriate role within a complex Programme, and to Angus McCabe, who provided an invaluable independent perspective as advisor to our team. We would also like to express our appreciation to the advisory group, whose names are listed in Appendix 4, and particularly to Richard Kemp as chair. Finally, we should thank the Joseph Rowntree Foundation itself for having the foresight to build evaluation in from the very beginning of the Programme.

The importance of the neighbourhood

Neighbourhoods are important. When the New Labour government came to power in 1997, it recognised that poverty and social exclusion tended to cluster in particular neighbourhoods. As part of its wider social exclusion programme, it developed a major neighbourhood renewal strategy to tackle this area-based disadvantage. Neighbourhoods have also been seen as an important staging post in more recent plans to improve service delivery, to give citizens in all parts of the country more power and to breathe new life into the democratic system. Working at neighbourhood level is seen as a way of getting closer to people, encouraging people to engage in public life and getting services to work more closely together. Although, for most of us, neighbourhoods may not be the centre of our existence, those of us who can afford to do so still select the neighbourhoods where we live very carefully. For some people, especially for children, older people and others who are not in work, the neighbourhood is still a significant point of reference.

Neighbourhood working has a long legacy. The past 40 years have seen a range of initiatives to decentralise service delivery and decision making through neighbourhood offices, neighbourhood councils, neighbourhood forums, neighbourhood policing and so on. There have been many inspiring stories over the years about how local residents have worked together to tackle local concerns, to develop a sense of 'community', to bring local parks and buildings back into use, to make their neighbourhood feel more safe and to set up all sorts of local activities.

Neighbourhood action is not the answer to everything. Many of the problems experienced in the most disadvantaged areas – job losses, changes in the housing market, loss of services – arise from decisions and developments far beyond the neighbourhood. But there is still much that can be done at neighbourhood level and there is a lot of experience now that can be shared between neighbourhoods and among service providers, business leaders and decision makers.

The past 40 years or so have seen a number of high-profile central government initiatives to support neighbourhood activity, especially in the most disadvantaged neighbourhoods. But there are many, many neighbourhoods that are not covered by special initiatives of this kind. In any case, these special initiatives have been time-limited, and central government, in England at least, is moving away from direct funding for neighbourhoods. If people in disadvantaged neighbourhoods are to be engaged in real change, this will increasingly depend on the local authority and local partners.

In this report, we share the experience of a four-year[1] programme that was set up to explore how neighbourhood activity could best be supported. The JRF Neighbourhood Programme worked with community-based organisations in 20 neighbourhoods

---

1 Includes the development phase.

JRF facilitator Trish McCue at a networking event with residents from Wales and the South West

across England, Scotland and Wales. These organisations were at very different stages of development and their access to resources varied considerably. Some were in neighbourhoods targeted by national regeneration programmes; others were in small pockets of disadvantage surrounded by relatively affluent areas with no access to special funding. The Programme provided a range of 'light touch' resources to these 20 neighbourhoods: a small funding pot (credit), support from experienced independent facilitators, networking opportunities and access to information. This not only offered an opportunity to test out the kinds of support that organisations at different stages of development might find useful; it also gave us a unique opportunity to look at the different challenges that community organisations face at different points as they try to get organised, get their neighbours in parts of the community involved, and engage with service providers and decision makers.

In this first chapter, we set out the policy context in each of the three countries where the Programme has been working and look at current policy developments. We also discuss some of the lessons from 40 years of neighbourhood initiatives and the challenges that these pose. Chapter 2 then describes the JRF Neighbourhood Programme in more detail: why it was set up, what it did, who was in it and what it offers to a wider audience.

The next three chapters summarise what we have learnt: Chapter 3 discusses the challenges that organisations face at neighbourhood level and some of the things that they have done to address these; Chapter 4 then looks at the added value the JRF Programme has brought and how it has helped organisations to tackle these challenges; Chapter 5 examines what this tells us about working effectively in neighbourhoods and how light touch support could work in future. Finally, Chapter 6 summarises the main findings and makes recommendations for policy and practice in all three countries. Throughout the text, we have provided examples of the work that Programme participants are doing across the three countries and, in the Resource sheets at the end, the reader will find some tools and pointers for working with neighbourhoods that we have found useful in, or that have emerged from, the work of the Programme.

The policy context

Area-based regeneration has a long history in the UK. In the 1960s and 1970s, area-based initiatives were seen as a vehicle for restoring a sense of community to populations who were rehoused as a result of slum clearance and other forms of redevelopment, for tackling urban unrest and racial tension and for tackling the persistent clustering of poverty and associated problems in particular neighbourhoods. Initiatives at that time emphasised the need for consultation, for rebuilding community and for coordination between different services – themes that are still familiar today.

With the election of the Conservative government in 1979, the emphasis changed to city-wide economic and physical regeneration, in the belief that wealth creation would trickle down to the less well off. But by the time the New Labour government was elected in 1997, a more community-based approach was already coming back into favour. This took shape in the form of the English National Strategy for Neighbourhood Renewal – with the neighbourhood acting as a focus both for participation and for the reshaping of service delivery. The devolved administrations meanwhile introduced their own area-based regeneration programmes: the Social Inclusion Partnerships (SIPs) in Scotland and the Communities First programme in Wales. While these brought their own distinctive emphasis, they reflected similar themes of community involvement, partnership and coordination between services.

England

New Labour policy on neighbourhoods arose out of its commitment to address social exclusion. Its ambitious National Strategy for Neighbourhood Renewal[2] was 'a 10 to 20 year plan to turn round poor neighbourhoods, to reduce dependency and to empower local communities' in order that 'no one' should be 'seriously disadvantaged by where they live' (see Box 1.1).

BOX 1.1 KEY ELEMENTS OF THE NATIONAL STRATEGY FOR NEIGHBOURHOOD RENEWAL

New Deal for Communities (NDC) – a 10-year project-based programme, investing significant funds in 39 localities.

Neighbourhood Management Pathfinders (NMPs) – a seven-year programme in 35 localities designed to lever change in mainstream services.

Neighbourhood Renewal Fund (NRF) – funding channelled through Local Strategic Partnerships (LSPs) in 88 priority local authority areas to support their Local Neighbourhood Renewal Strategies .

Neighbourhood Wardens – a three-year pilot programme in 84 neighbourhoods.

In addition, a **Single Community Programme** in each of the 88 NRF priority areas provided infrastructure support to local organisations and a route to influence the LSP through a Community Empowerment Network in each locality.

The Strategy also included the formation of a **National Community Forum**, which brought a small group of experienced residents from neighbourhood level together to advise government on neighbourhood renewal policy.

---

[2] SEU (2001)

Despite the commitment to a long-term strategy, recent years have seen policy move away from an emphasis on targeted special initiatives to tackling disadvantage within a more comprehensive local government framework.

First, there has been a shift from project-based special funding initiatives to a neighbourhood management approach whose delivery depends on cooperation between mainstream service providers at a neighbourhood level. Through mainstreaming, central government aims to ensure that the hundreds of millions of pounds tied up in mainstream services are harnessed to the benefit of the most disadvantaged neighbourhoods.

Second is the central government commitment to devolve powers and resources to local authority level, with the possibility of further devolution, through parish councils and similar bodies, confirmed in the Local Government White Paper published in late 2006.[3] Funding for neighbourhood renewal has already been devolved to local level and subsumed within the 'safer and stronger communities block' of the Local Area Agreement (LAA) that is now a requirement of every local authority.[4] The focus on disadvantaged neighbourhoods is currently retained through a 'neighbourhood element'. However, there are proposals to give local authorities greater flexibility in the use of these funds, through dissolving the current four blocks and combining their funding in a single pot.

Community engagement was central to the English national strategy and the recent White Paper confirms the importance of working closely with citizens and communities. It confirms and extends the requirements for local authorities to ensure the participation of local communities in the shaping and delivery of LAAs and other aspects of their work.

Neighbourhood management in action: Chris Parsons chairing a meeting of Scarborough's Eastfield Neighbourhood Partnership

---

[3] DCLG (2006a)

[4] LAAs are three-year agreements between government, the local authority and its major delivery partners in an area (working through LSPs) that set out the agreed priorities and targets for the area. They are based on Sustainable Community Strategies, likewise agreed between partners, which set out the broader vision and priorities for the area.

It also introduces a variety of new mechanisms for citizens to hold government to account and participate in governance, while reinforcing the role of ward councillors as key intermediaries between the citizen and the state. It also commits government to continued support for the empowerment of local people and communities, building on Together We Can, an initiative developed across government to enable people to engage with public bodies and influence the decisions that affect their communities.

Sustainable communities policies in England provide a wider context for the National Strategy for Neighbourhood Renewal (see Appendix 5). English policy is also encouraging mixed tenure to introduce greater social diversity to neighbourhoods characterised by multiple deprivation.

Scotland

Scottish policy for regeneration is encompassed within a social justice framework and included within a comprehensive Community Planning policy (see Box 1.2).

BOX 1.2 NEIGHBOURHOOD RENEWAL IN SCOTLAND

Thirteen Working for Communities (WFC) partnership pathfinders were set up in 1998 to test innovative local service delivery and budgeting in disadvantaged neighbourhoods. These gave way in 2002 to 48 SIPs of which 34 were area-based and 14 thematic, each with a Community Empowerment Fund designed to strengthen community participation. A Better Neighbourhood Services Fund, covering the period 2001–05 was also introduced in 12 pathfinder areas to improve services for people living in disadvantaged areas.

These two funds have now given way to **Community Planning** (see main text), although a three-year, £318 million **Community Regeneration Fund (CRF)** was introduced in 2004, targeted at the 15% most disadvantaged neighbourhoods in Scotland. To secure funding, Community Planning Partnerships (CPPs) set out how they intend to use the CRF alongside their own resources to deliver specific regeneration outcomes through three-year Regeneration Outcome Agreements. However, CRF areas do not correspond to the new local CPPs, despite the stated intention to rationalise partnerships. A three-year **Community Voices Programme** was introduced in 2005 to support CPPs to deliver community engagement (see main text).

The Scottish Parliament anticipated the English move from targeted special initiatives to a more comprehensive local governance framework by some two years. The 2003 Local Government in Scotland Act established the Community Planning system – a statutory framework of duties for institutional stakeholders to engage with citizens in developing a Community Plan to improve the delivery of services and meet the aspirations of communities. Unlike England (through the LSPs), there is no statutory obligation to involve communities at local authority level, but what the Scottish Act does include is a duty to engage at sub-authority level, where citizens are expected to engage in local Community Planning Partnerships. Community Planning is Scotland-wide and not confined to disadvantaged neighbourhoods, although there are still some special funding mechanisms for such neighbourhoods, through, for example, the CRF (see Box 1.2). There is also a Community Voices Programme that supports community engagement activity in the most disadvantaged areas in Scotland.

The Scottish Executive's recent Regeneration Policy Statement[5] focuses on economic growth through physical regeneration and echoes the English interest in encouraging

---

5   Scottish Executive (2006)

Shopping in Glasgow's East Pollokshields, where local groups have joined forces behind a Community Plan

mixed tenure. The Executive is encouraging developers and registered social landlords (RSLs) to build for sale or rent in the most deprived neighbourhoods, as well as investing in new housing in support of local regeneration priorities and introducing housing renewal areas to tackle poor and declining housing standards.

Wales

A concern with social justice has also been at the heart of Welsh regeneration policy, in recognition of the acute social disadvantage experienced throughout Wales.[6]

BOX 1.3 NEIGHBOURHOOD RENEWAL IN WALES

The Welsh Assembly inherited 16 area-based **People in Communities** programmes from the Welsh Office, and the generally positive evaluation of this programme led to **Communities First**, a 10-year programme through which special funds are disbursed to 132 neighbourhoods and 10 communities of interest. Communities are expected to play a key role in the cross-sectoral partnerships that support the local Communities First programmes – at least equal to that of any other group – on a 'three thirds' principle of one third statutory, one third community and one third split between the voluntary sector and business.

The flagship programme for neighbourhood renewal in Wales is Communities First, which has so far focused on capacity building, community empowerment and building social capital. It is therefore less prescriptive or target-driven than the equivalent programmes in England and, to some extent, Scotland, and although it is focused on 'bending' the mainstream, the interim evaluation of Communities First is that this has yet to be achieved.[7] The attempts to rationalise and focus partnerships that have characterised English and

---

[6]   Adamson (2006)

[7]   Welsh Assembly Government (2006a)

An informal get together on Gellideg estate, one of Wales's Communities First areas

Scottish policy in relation to LAAs and Community Planning, respectively, have not been replicated to the same extent in Wales. However, following the Beecham review of public service delivery,the Assembly proposes to introduce local service boards and local service agreements to encourage joint delivery and more pooling of resources.[8] There is not the same extent of devolution as in the other two countries – civil servants will be on the public service boards and there will be a strong geographical role for ministers. There is also a commitment to a citizen focus in contrast to what Beecham identified as a 'consumer focus' in England, and to being more ambitious about engaging citizens in the design, delivery and improvement of services – an action plan for public engagement and the role of the voluntary and community sector is planned.

The National Housing Strategy for Wales[9] recommends that planners encourage mixed tenure in future communities, but there is not the same emphasis on mixed tenure in existing deprived neighbourhoods as in the other two countries.

---

[8] Welsh Assembly Government (2006a, 2006b)
[9] Welsh Assembly Government (2006c)

Young people from Llanharan who were involved in Cardiff Museum's On Common Ground arts project

European programmes

These programmes in the three countries also operate alongside European programmes focusing on disadvantaged neighbourhoods, the URBAN Programme and Objective 1 programmes in particular. However, funding from these sources is shortly due to come to an end in many parts of Britain and, with the need to focus on the accession states, the European Union is unlikely to be a significant future source of investment. Where it does continue, its increased focus on strategic and regional developments is likely to impact on support for community-based regeneration activities.

BOX 1.4 EXAMPLES OF FUNDING CONCERNS

There are more than 700 posts in councils for voluntary service in Wales that are funded by Europe, and which therefore risk being lost as Objective 1 funding is reduced and reorganised. Three regions in England have also benefited from Objective 1 funding and there are major concerns about how the neighbourhood-level infrastructure development that has been supported so far will continue.

In England, concerns about funding are heightened by the devolution of significant neighbourhood renewal resources to local authority level and, more significantly, the loss of Single Regeneration Budget (SRB) funding, which has been significant in pump priming and maintaining projects at neighbourhood level for more than a decade. The remnants of SRB will expire in 2008.

The future of neighbourhoods

Overall, while there is a commitment to some form of sub-local governance to engage citizens and focus service delivery, the extent of likely devolution is less clear. But whatever policy dictates, the reality is that the neighbourhood level will continue to be an important space for people to come together and take action around the issues that most concern them, especially in the less prosperous areas, where people have fewer choices about where they live and the services they use. There is already a considerable body of knowledge about what works and what does not at this level. Successive evaluations have emphasised the need for:

- flexibility – one size does not fit all
- building on what is already there – new programmes need to fit into the existing landscape
- time – for trust to be developed, skills and capacity to be built and the foundations of partnership to be laid down
- sustainable resources for participation
- capacity building among partners as well as communities
- consistency and coordination at national level
- neighbourhood action to be linked into wider policies

However, they also suggest that there is still some way to go before community organisations at neighbourhood level will feel that they are full partners in neighbourhood renewal. Many public authorities still do not have clear devolved mechanisms in place to engage people in policy at neighbourhood level or to ensure that mainstream departments can respond to neighbourhood priorities. And there are tensions between the emphasis on community engagement in determining priorities for the neighbourhood and contrary pressures that urge economies of scale. Rationalisation has, for example, been a strong force in the provision of housing, where despite policies to increase choice of providers, there is a strong trend for housing associations to merge and grow.

A corner shop in the Broad Street neighbourhood in Swindon

Some of the key challenges that need to be addressed if more power is to be devolved to citizens are:

- How do we define neighbourhoods that are meaningful to people? In England, the NMP evaluation suggests that the 'ideal' size of a neighbourhood is between 5,000 and 15,000 households. The Young Foundation develops this further (see Box 1.5).

BOX 1.5 LEVELS OF NEIGHBOURHOOD

A recent Young Foundation paper says that there is a general consensus among practitioners that 'neighbourhood' refers mainly to areas of around 1,000 to 10,000 people (although with smaller and larger outliers, such as hamlets and market towns).[10] It goes on, however, to suggest three layers of neighbourhood that are relevant in different ways for different issues 'but which make both objective and subjective sense in most contexts'. The layers are:

- streets and blocks of about 50–300 people, where association, informal social control and mutual aid are key governance tools;
- 'home neighbourhoods' or 'proximity neighbourhoods' of around 500–2,000 people bringing together a few blocks – a scale at which Neighbourhood Warden schemes often make sense;
- public or strategic neighbourhoods of 4,000–15,000 people where more structured governance starts to make sense.

How should this translate into policy design and practice?

- Despite many different policies encouraging participation, relatively few people get involved at neighbourhood level. Does this matter and, if so, what is it realistic to expect?
- A neighbourhood focus can overlook communities of identity that are invisible at that level. Everything we read nowadays reminds us of increasing diversity – how can this be reconciled with cohesion and will it be possible to resist fragmentation?
- Despite years of community participation programmes, there are still pockets of resistance within and across the public sector. How can these be overcome?
- How does the drive for greater participation fit with the formal representation system? In England, ward councillors are being given significant new powers and being urged to become community leaders. What will be their relationship with residents who have taken on a leadership role locally?
- With the exception of Wales, most regeneration programmes are targeted at relatively few neighbourhoods. Although social exclusion is concentrated spatially, the fact remains that there is still as much poverty and deprivation outside these neighbourhoods as within – in rural as well as urban areas. How can we find ways of supporting the many neighbourhoods that will never be beneficiaries of targeted funding, whether this comes from central or local government?
- Devolving power down to the locality is welcome, setting a premium on neighbourhood choice and local priorities, but it can lead to a postcode lottery. What role is it appropriate for central government to play in ensuring minimum standards of support and provision?

---

[10] Hilder (2005)

A street in Eastfield, Scarborough

Meanwhile, the reconfiguration of European funding, alongside – in England – the devolution of significant neighbourhood renewal resources to the local level, creates cause for concern. While this devolution has the potential to tailor funds to local needs and circumstances, the drive that has come from the centre for genuine community engagement will now depend very much on the understanding in each local authority and/ or LSP of the resources and commitment that this entails.

2

The JRF Neighbourhood Programme: a 'light touch' learning network

The Neighbourhood Programme was the first of the JRF Policy and Practice Development programmes. It was established in 2002 with the following aims:

> To enable twenty communities, starting from their own agenda, to gain access to: knowledge and information, and the skills to apply this in their own neighbourhoods; the support they need in this process from peer networks and other agencies; and power, at whatever appropriate level, in order to unlock barriers to their successful engagement with neighbourhood renewal.

The Programme offered small amounts of funding (credit), support from an independent facilitator, opportunities to network nationally and regionally, access to information through a website and JRF publications, the status of being associated with a national programme and opportunities to contribute to JRF national events. As the Programme got under way, it also developed a brokerage element. The Programme has been supported by a full-time Programme manager and an advisory group. Evaluation was built in from the beginning.

The rationale for the Programme

The Joseph Rowntree Foundation has a long history of influencing social policy through research, debate and lobbying and through accessible and widely distributed *Findings*. In the late 1990s internal discussions within JRF led to a shift in emphasis away from 'pure' research and towards programmes that intervene with practitioners or in communities as an additional means of influencing policy and practice. The Neighbourhood Programme was one outcome of this.

The Programme sought to establish a 'learning network', which would promote inter-organisational learning through:

- networks of mutual support between community organisations;
- transfer of knowledge of 'what works';
- generating new knowledge and ideas through networking and dialogue;
- access to local power holders.

This 'learning network' model was driven by three perceptions within JRF.

Planting out shrubs in Caia Park, Wrexham: volunteers brightening up an area of public open space

First, although a lot of knowledge exists in community organisations, it is scattered widely. JRF believed that bringing Programme participants together in networks would lead to sharing experience and joint problem solving.

Second, community development and other professionals have built up knowledge about the way things change in communities and community organisations. While some of this knowledge is embodied in JRF research and publications, it is not necessarily accessible to community organisations. This Programme was intended to provide a way of transferring this knowledge to community organisations.

Third, JRF itself is well connected into national and local decision-making systems. It wanted these connections to be used to improve the position of community organisations in relation to their local power holders.

An additional point of interest arising from this particular programme relates to JRF's role as a direct funder of community organisations. This provided the opportunity for the Foundation to provide a positive model for the relationship between funder and communities and to test out ways of managing the challenges this power relationship brings.

What the Programme offers

The Programme worked with 20 community-based organisations at different stages of development and working in different operational contexts. Working with this range of groups and organisations over a four-year period offered an opportunity:

- to support individual community organisations to achieve their own aims, using a range of methods of intervention;
- to generate valuable learning and knowledge about community strengths and achievements, relationships between communities and local stakeholders, and neighbourhood renewal;
- to test out how far different kinds of support and networking opportunities can help communities to overcome the barriers they face (both internal and external);
- to contribute to policy and practice in neighbourhood renewal (in keeping with the JRF mission).

The resources that the Programme offered are summarised in Box 2.1 overleaf.

BOX 2.1 SUMMARY OF RESOURCES AVAILABLE WITHIN THE NEIGHBOURHOOD PROGRAMME

- *Action planning* – a planning framework and evaluation guidelines were produced to help organisations develop and review action plans.
- *Development support (facilitation)* – five highly experienced people were selected as independent, regionally based facilitators. They brought a mix of community development, project management, academic, mentoring and consultancy skills and were allocated a number of days to undertake planning and development support with each organisation over the lifetime of the Programme. (This varied between 15 and 30 days over the three years of the Programme, determined by anticipated support needs and existing support resources.).
- *Credit* – a small funding pot for the organisations to use at their discretion. Money was available 'up front' and could be spent at any time (ie it was not restricted to financial years). Some organisations received £10,000, some £5,000 and some (three organisations) nothing, again determined by existing resources available.
- *Networking* – opportunities were provided to enable organisations to learn from one another through twice-yearly two-day networking events, and through regionally based workshops. Organisations were also encouraged to visit each other.
- *Joint (cross-neighbourhood) projects* on fundraising, community engagement, diversity and relationships with power holders – each bringing together a selection of organisations for workshops and case study interviews in order to pool promising practice.
- *Access to information* – the JRF Programme manager acted as a source of topical information sharing and as an enquiry point for organisations. A website was developed to share learning from within the programme and signpost to other sources of research and information (from within JRF and outside).
- *Brokerage* – mediation between participating organisations and other community-based organisations or local power holders such as the local authority.
- *Kitemarking* – organisations were able to use the JRF name to raise their profile and could request letters signed by Lord Best to validate their involvement with the programme.
- *A national platform* – organisations were supported to promote their activities at national conferences, and to make links with the wider world of regeneration; JRF also held workshops in each of the three countries to share learning with local authorities.

Rhianon Passmore from Ty Sign (Newport) and Derrick Purdue (one of JRF's evaluators) share a joke at a JRF regional networking event

Who participated in the Programme

There were several stages to the selection of organisations. Rather than openly advertise, JRF used its own networks to nominate 60 organisations in five regions. Nominators drawn from both statutory and voluntary and community sectors were asked to suggest organisations and provide accompanying information about them and why they should be included. Forty of these organisations were asked to apply and 20 were accepted. Some of the applications came from the organisations themselves; others from support workers. The selections were made by an advisory group, made up of people involved in policy and practice across the three countries (see Appendix 4 for membership). In deciding how many organisations to select, advisory group members had to balance the need to have enough organisations to make it a national Programme with the need to ensure that the number of organisations chosen could be meaningfully involved with a limited budget. Most of those involved feel that the settled number of 20 was appropriate and manageable within the resources of the Programme.

The 20 organisations are described in Appendix 1. They were chosen to provide a sufficiently diverse sample for a national programme (within resource constraints), with a wide regional spread: four organisations in each of five regions – Scotland, Wales, Yorkshire and Humber, West Midlands and South West England. This distribution allows for some comparison between the national/regional structures in Scotland and Wales on the one hand, and the English regions on the other.

The organisations included were at different stages of development and based in different types of neighbourhood – some were community led; others had paid workers. They ranged from informal organisations of volunteers to well-established organisations with 70-plus employees. Using information provided by the Programme participants, the evaluation team classified them according to four stages of development (see Table 2.1).

Adding the finishing touches: volunteers complete a garden of rest next to a church in Boscombe. The work was supported by Boscombe Working Community Partnership

Table 2.1 Neighbourhood organisations by stage of development

Stage 1	Just starting out as community organisations	8 organisations	Recipients of help
Stage 2	Service delivery organisations, engaging with potential partners	4 organisations	
Stage 3	Beginning to take strategic leadership role in the neighbourhood	4 organisations	
Stage 4	Mature organisations that could share experience and with interest in national profile	4 organisations	Providers of experience and practice

This was an initial snapshot of the community organisations and, as time has moved on, some of the organisations have moved from one stage to another. Nor is development always linear – some have ebbed and flowed. But, whatever the stage of development, most of the organisations have been both recipients of help and providers of practice. Chapter 5 will reflect further on what we have learnt about organisational life cycles.

Once the 20 organisations had been confirmed as full members, they were asked to produce a detailed proposal and a three-year action plan in order to determine access to credit and facilitation time. The facilitators were given the task of encouraging and supporting them in this process.

Learning from the Programme's start-up phase

Selection: open or closed?

The Joseph Rowntree Foundation was successful in attracting both a wide geographical spread of organisations and a range of organisations in terms of size, capacity and history. The direct involvement of community activists is seen as a particularly significant aspect of the Programme. However, the outcomes of the process suggest that more could have been done to encourage applications from black and minority ethnic (BME) communities.

'I felt the selection process was rushed and unsatisfactory in terms of attracting and identifying a suitable range of groups – for example, there are very few BME organisations taking part and I am not entirely convinced that all the groups are firmly rooted in their communities…. Otherwise, I felt the process was fair in that the same criteria were applied to all applications, and that groups were given a lot of support in making their applications.' (Member of the Programme advisory group).

The views of advisory group members involved in the selection process varied – some did not feel that it was robust enough; others disagreed:

'… certainly the process of identifying neighbourhoods was robust and democratic.'

'[I] would have preferred an open application process, rather than nominations, had it been practicable, which it wasn't!'

'I certainly hope we learnt that selection from paper alone is not enough – we should have visited areas to get a more hands-on knowledge of the projects.'

These mixed views illustrate how difficult it is to get the right balance between the needs of participating organisations and a programme's sponsor in establishing a 'fair' and effective selection process. They also highlight the difficulty of developing clear selection criteria at the start of a new experimental programme where there are inevitable uncertainties about how it will develop.

Development time

The setting-up process also took longer than expected. Any new programme has to balance the need to allow time for development with the need to get the show on the road and make visible progress. But even though JRF research has consistently criticised the lack of development time in government programmes, they still had to learn this lesson first hand. However, unlike many other funding programmes, the Foundation was flexible enough to respond by extending the Programme's life by a year in order to accommodate the time it (always) takes to get programmes up and running.

Hanging out in Ty Sign, Caerphilly: two friends stop for a catch up

Action planning: flexibility or accountability?

The action planning process was somewhat controversial. JRF had to face the challenges of any funder in balancing flexibility with accountability for the investment it was planning to make, but a number of the organisations found themselves disappointed to begin with. Some of the smaller organisations felt that JRF was proving to be no different from other funders in the bureaucratic hurdles it created: "To start with action planning was a pain". For larger organisations, meanwhile, this was yet another plan among the many they had to prepare for other funders. Imposing this process at the beginning meant that, in some cases, the period of gaining trust and developing an effective working relationship between facilitators and the neighbourhood organisations was lengthened.

In addition, it was not clear whether the plan was for the group, the neighbourhood or simply for their use of JRF resources, and different organisations and facilitators interpreted it differently. However as the Programme progressed and it turned into a tool for annual review, the role of the action plan became clearer. As we shall see in Chapter 4, many organisations – especially those who were new to the whole concept – were to find this process extremely useful.

In conclusion, the development of the Neighbourhood Programme was in some ways – for example, the changes made to the selection process and the time extension – quite organic, yet other aspects were fairly controlled, for example, the action planning process. The extent of flexibility within the programme is something we shall return to in the following chapters.

What happens in neighbourhoods

At the start of the Programme, in their applications and initial networking meetings, participating organisations were asked to identify the problems and issues they faced in their neighbourhoods and what was needed to bring about change. These can broadly be summarised under the following headings:

- insufficient analysis of local problems and assets
- limited engagement of local residents
- the need to build organisational capacity and leadership
- divisions and fragmentation within the neighbourhood
- lack of influence with local power holders
- difficulties in securing sustainable funding

We used the first five of these headings to help participating organisations to think through the action they needed to make a difference (see Resource sheet A). Networking meetings allowed us to explore further issues of organisational capacity and leadership, while the last four of these issues also formed the basis of four 'joint projects' – each bringing together a selection of organisations for workshops and case study interviews in order to pool promising practice – which provided us with an opportunity to explore in more detail the nature of the problems and how they could be tackled.

These are issues that will be familiar to many readers. In this chapter we discuss in more detail what we learnt about how they were experienced in the JRF neighbourhoods and describe some of the ways in which organisations in the Programme addressed them. Although few of their approaches were completely new, these were the kind of ideas that many of the smaller organisations in particular were looking for. Most participants valued the sharing of this experience and were eager to learn from others.

Knowing your neighbourhood

An analysis of local needs, problems and assets is an important place to start if organisations are to be effective and strategic. But, unless they are part of a programme that demands some kind of plan, few organisations do start here. They are more likely to get going because of a pressing problem and then the sheer momentum of day-to-day demands takes over. Indeed, for many participants in the Programme, action planning was something new.

Most of the larger, more professionalised organisations in the Programme and those who were already in receipt of funding had some kind of plan. Indeed, several of our organisations had to prepare a number of parallel plans to satisfy different funders' needs, but these were as likely to be dictated by the funders' priorities as by local needs, and they

Part of the transformation: a commercial development in Castle Vale, complete with public art

resisted the need for yet another plan. Indeed, the more professionalised an organisation became, the more likely it was to engage in some form of planning.

BOX 3.1 THE VALUE OF PLANNING

Castle Vale has been totally transformed over the past 12 years. What has been achieved is truly astonishing; where previously Castle Vale was a place people were queuing up to leave, it is now an area where people want to move to and raise their families. However, the continued regeneration of Castle Vale will not happen by accident.

The Neighbourhood Partnership Board has just approved an evidence-based Neighbourhood Plan, 'Making Castle Vale an even better place to live', that will drive the continued regeneration of Castle Vale. The plan addresses issues that matter most to residents, such as litter, graffiti, dog mess and anti-social behaviour as well as 'closing the gap' issues, such as health and worklessness, that are important for the area's sustained improvement. The plan makes links both with the Constituency Community Plan and Birmingham's Strategic Plan.

Local strategic planning at local authority and sub-local level demands a comprehensive analysis of local needs and assets. This has been the case for some time in Scotland, and our four Scottish neighbourhoods were gearing up to the Community Planning agenda, so that they could become key players in the planning process. In some other areas, a community safety audit has provided the first hard evidence of what local needs are. In England, a robust analysis of local needs is likely to become increasingly important in future if neighbourhood organisations are to gain both funds and influence in their authority's Sustainable Community Plan and LAA.

Ian Cooke of Pilton Partnership, and JRF facilitator Michael Carley, out and about in Pilton, Edinburgh

Community profiling and planning gives neighbourhood organisations credibility when dealing with decision makers. It also encourages organisations to become more strategic. But it can address many of the other issues that organisations raised at the beginning of the Programme. Integrate, in Todmorden, used a door-to-door survey of local Asian families not only to find out what they wanted for their own community, but also to connect them to existing organisations and help them to feel part of the wider community. The example from the Pilton Partnership in Box 3.2 illustrates how the planning process can be a creative and engaging approach to community engagement.

BOX 3.2 THE PILTON PARTNERSHIP: ENGAGING LOCAL PEOPLE THROUGH PLANNING

Faced with the introduction of new Community Planning structures in Scotland, the **Pilton Partnership** organised a residential community conference, to involve local people in reviewing partnership working and planning for the future. The partnership used a variety of creative and participatory methods to engage existing activists and the wider community. A series of eight consultation events began with a slide show illustrating some of the changes in the area, with participants using electronic voting pads to respond to a set of questions relating to perceived improvements in different aspects of local services and the quality of life.

These were followed by a residential community conference of 48 community activists, who identified priority issues and how the community should respond to the Community Planning agenda. The programme involved:

- sharing personal experiences of community initiatives through songs, drama and artwork;
- putting the SIP on trial in a court case drama;
- asking activists to complete time priority circles to reflect on how they spent their time and what lessons could be drawn in relation to effective use of time and widening community involvement;
- mapping existing community groups and activist involvement in the neighbourhood, analysing strengths and weaknesses of groups and structures;
- collages of the community's vision for the future and the steps necessary to achieve these aims;
- considering what Community Planning would mean for the SIP and how the community should engage with this agenda.

Proposals were developed for Community Councils, four of which have now been established. The community is now well prepared for Community Planning and able to hold others in the Community Planning structures to account. The review activities have provided an important opportunity for breaking down some of the barriers between generations through the successful involvement of young people in the community conference and highlighted the importance of regularly reviewing community involvement structures.

Engaging with the wider local community

This Programme made us aware just how fragile many community organisations are, reliant on the energies of two or three people and with few resources. In these situations, one individual can make or break an organisation and a key individual moving on can be a major crisis. Some of the problems experienced are common: "too many moaners, not enough 'doers'"; "recruiting volunteers is very difficult and very slow". Others are more specific but are certainly not unique: "we lost half of the original committee – no out-of-pocket expenses"; "the chair ... is a bully ... people leave because of this"; "our leading volunteer died".

Developing a large enough pool of active residents is important for many reasons. It increases the energies and resources available to organisations in the neighbourhood. It ensures that local organisations are responding to local needs and aspirations. It also gives a group legitimacy when it is dealing with outsiders. How often have we heard local authorities complain about 'the usual suspects' or say that a group is 'unrepresentative'?

But involving people is not easy. Small organisations may lack the confidence to go out and engage more people. Or they may not see the need – some are essentially social in nature, a group of friends who enjoy working together, which is fine so long as they do not then claim to speak on behalf of the wider neighbourhood. They may have got used to doing things on their own. Or they may simply not know how to get more people on board. Participants also spoke about leaders who put the damper on any new initiative: "they've seen it all, done it all and nothing works". Leaders who have invested a lot of time and energy in a neighbourhood over the years can find it difficult to delegate or allow others in, let alone take advice from outsiders. But, equally, their neighbours may be happy to let them to get on with the job.

Involvement can also be a problem for the larger, more successful community organisations. Even where neighbourhood activity involves a lot of people to start with, as it becomes more professionalised and has to satisfy the needs of its funders, it can lose touch with its roots. The Pilton Partnership has a long history of community development and has a dedicated community development team, but it still recognises the need to 'give the extra effort' required to continually bring new people in.

Organisations in the Programme have tackled these issues in a number of ways, which are examined in detail on pages 24-29.

Away they go! Balloons being released at the opening of Ty Sign's community shop

Facilities

Eight organisations in the Programme have their own premises. A community base is important in getting residents involved in the group, attracting volunteers and enquiries. Local community buildings act as a 'hub' for the neighbourhood – somewhere to identify with. They give the group a visible presence.

BOX 3.3 THE VALUE OF A COMMUNITY BUILDING

Ty Sign Local Communities Partnership is a small community group based on an estate lacking community facilities. It developed a new focal point for the community in the form of a community shop/cafe. The shop is located in a row of shops and leased from the council at a peppercorn rent.

The shop has been opening all day and some evenings, putting on a funded learning programme so that the group can also attract paid lettings, with refurbishment under way. It has been used to bring a whole range of new services onto the estate including a community nurse seeing 30-40 patients a month, Careers Wales, and Working Links, which works with single parents to get them back into employment. The group also uses the building as a base to run 50+ bingo, summer play schemes for children and drug and alcohol awareness sessions with Fusion, and for an energetic youth group to meet and organise events such as two community festivals.

The community cafe is run as a coffee shop and acts as a community meeting place. Run by volunteers, it is well established and open every day. A 'cook and eat club' is planned to introduce healthy and cheap eating options, especially for single parents and young people living on their own.

Ty Sign Local Communities Partnership is now extending into the property next door, setting up a learning centre and an IT suite, which can be closed off for teaching. Current users include the youth group whose success is striking. Within a year of starting out (and without the support of a paid youth worker), the group has become a model for other initiatives in South Wales: "The simple factor which other community groups have difficulty in grasping, is that the Ty Sign youngsters have been given the freedom, support (and a little funding from JRF) to manage their own affairs".

However, buildings are not always an asset, and a centre can be vulnerable if it is not owned by the group – one of the participating organisations lost its base when the local authority terminated the lease in favour of one of its own projects. Buildings leased at a peppercorn rent from a local authority can suddenly become a burden if the authority changes its charging policy. Buildings can also be a burden if they need a lot of work to renovate or maintain them. On the other hand, one Programme organisation is in the position of having been so successful with its building that it has filled it to capacity and now has difficulty accommodating everything it has set in motion.

Celebratory events

Having fun is an essential part of getting people involved – several organisations have put on celebratory events including food, especially as a way of getting minority ethnic organisations or young people involved. Work talk or community problems are put to one side as people socialise and enjoy a meal together.

BOX 3.4 CELEBRATORY EVENTS

Broad Street has held two successful multicultural days of food and dance, each attracting over 200 people. One way of attracting people to the events was for each member of the group personally to invite 10 people they knew. It helped, too, that, before the second event, the group had recruited new BME members who took a lead in organising the event. The enthusiastic leadership provided by new members and the informal nature of both events were major factors in their success.

In Todmorden, a multicultural food festival, held by **Integrate** in conjunction with a local SRB scheme drew in more than 200 people, including the mayor, and secured lots of positive publicity in the town. Along with a programme of summer activities it raised lots of interest in the community. They also held an Eid party in Todmorden Town Hall, which brought in 800 people.

A flagship project of the **Boothtown Community Partnership** is its successful multicultural Food and Dance Community Festival. Established in 2003, and in part a response to increasing British National Party activity in the area, it aims to provide a visual community celebration and public expression of diverse culture. The Partnership is committed to the festival as a permanent event and has forged links with another festival group in the town.

Front-room meetings

Joining an existing group can be difficult. Residents need a variety of informal ways into engagement with the people they know and trust, especially those who feel marginalised or isolated within the neighbourhood. In Malvern, the community development worker recruited some local residents to invite their friends round for an informal discussion in their own homes. This worked well, for a number of reasons. First there was no distance to travel. Second, residents were with people they knew well. They were invited by word of mouth – as one of the facilitators said: "It's people that bring people, not posters or leaflets". Third, the provision of some simple statistics and facts about the area gave residents a place to start and endorsed their own views of the problems on the estate.

The Mayor of Halifax – and Zulu dancers – get into a knees-up at the Boothtown Festival

BOX 3.5 MALVERN'S FRONT-ROOM MEETINGS

In **Malvern**, it became clear that an existing group was not going to provide the basis for more widespread engagement. So the community worker asked a number of her existing contacts whether they would be willing to host an informal meeting in their front room to talk about what local people felt about where they lived and what they thought should be happening there. Each meeting involved five or six people and they were invited by word of mouth. Careful preparation and expert facilitation helped to ensure the meetings ran well and those who attended felt they were treated as 'experts'. The project had a big map of the estate and could overlay it with statistics provided by the police and other agencies. This gave the front-room meetings some real evidence to work on. Each meeting produced at least one person who was willing to provide street-level input to the operational and strategy groups that were to be set up on the estate.

However, while this can be a good way of reaching all parts of the community, it is important then to move on to the next step of bringing these organisations together and building bridges between them (see 'Working with diversity' on page 33).

Working with children and young people

The need to reach out to young people was a priority for many of the organisations in the Programme when they started. This is particularly important in a climate where any group of young people gathering in a public place tends to be seen as a community safety risk. Working with young people not only addresses the generational gap. It breeds the active citizens of the future and can help to get parents involved.

Boothtown Youth Forum: baby reality session

BOX 3.6 BOOTHTOWN YOUTH FORUM

With a small space inside the community partnership building and a small grant from the youth service, two local residents have established a very successful youth forum and 'drop-in', and illustrated the value of young people's capacity and involvement.

After much discussion with youth workers and community partnership members, and through talking with local young people, "We had a meeting with young people, gave them big pieces of paper and asked them what they wanted, their expectations of us and set some ground rules".

The following week, young people turned up at the Boothtown Community Partnership building, and they have continued to 'drop in' once a week ever since. Since March 2005, 109 young people have registered, most are 14- to 15-year-olds: "[they have] realised they have somewhere to go". There is a mix of planned and informal activities, which have included a sexual health session, a baby reality session, a beauty makeover session ("you should have seen the boys!"), crafts nights and open discussion sessions. The Youth Forum is keen to repeat its successful trip to Alton Towers, which resulted in team building, and trust and group development.

There is still more to do – the young people keep asking for more sessions and the potential for young people's influence over local developments, for example, use of public space, the community festival and the partnership itself, has not been fully realised. This is primarily due to a lack of resources such as space, money and time – the two community volunteers already commit an average of 40 to 50 voluntary hours a month.

Llanharan Community Development Project (CDP) has recently acquired funding from the Heritage Lottery Fund Young Roots strand for young people to make and sail traditional Welsh coracles, including using traditional tools.

Norma Thompson, Nazma Ramruttun and Neil Poulton from Broad Street in Swindon, with Trish McCue from the JRF Programme

Providing services to 'new communities'

Some Programme participants have provided services to marginalised groups, for example, language classes and bilingual advice for refugees and migrant workers. St Pauls Unlimited and Caia Park Partnership also provide translation services that are highly valued, but finding the resources to keep them going is a problem for both organisations.

BOX 3.7 BRIDGING COMMUNITIES

Caia Park Partnership (CPP) has been providing English language courses and bilingual advice for new migrants, mainly from Eastern European countries. Language is a big barrier for migrant workers, and English courses are delivered at the Partnership offices by the Workers Educational Association and attended by over 70 Polish and Portuguese people. While language courses are available elsewhere, it was only CPP who responded to the huge increase in demand. People from all over Wrexham came to CPP because the Polish people who live in Caia Park felt comfortable there and recommended it. The Partnership does an initial assessment of people applying for courses, which means that they can start to address other issues at an early stage. The Partnership's provision also includes interpretation and translation services. New migrants can get help with signing up children to schools at the start of the autumn term, referrals to local GPs, contact with a health visitor, reassuring contact with the local community police officer, and advice on a range of other issues. It has not been easy to find funding for this work and only a small part of the funding comes from the local authority who undoubtedly benefit from this provision.

In **Broad Street,** a local resident from St Helena has set up the St Helena Trust to help his newly arrived compatriots to acquire the official credentials they need to work in the UK.

Community newsletters

Lack of communication within the neighbourhood is a common problem. St Pauls Unlimited described how it used a milk float to communicate with the whole community. Getting positive coverage in the local newspaper is important and several of the smaller organisations in the Programme were particularly interested in finding out how to set up their own community newspapers – a workshop was set up at one of the JRF regional meetings to share experience. They can play an important role in improving local communication and helping people to feel 'in touch'. And news produced by residents for residents has a particular value in building local identity and confidence.

> 'At their best, small local newspapers can give people the information they need to start changing their communities for the better.'

Community newspapers may seem like an obvious thing for a group to do. But they can be highly variable in quality and difficult to maintain – they take a lot of energy to produce regularly on a long-term basis. They need expertise and resources but are hard to fund. In one JRF neighbourhood, a local social enterprise had been set up to generate jobs and income for the community.

Smina Akhtar and colleagues in East Pollokshields mull over ideas for their community newsletter

BOX 3.8 A MEDIA ENTERPRISE IN GLASGOW

Pollokshields East Partnership picked up on the lack of communication in their neighbourhood from a community survey. As a result, it looked for funding to establish a new project called Radius Glasgow, one of whose objectives would be to set up a community newsletter.

A journalist and local resident had been working on plans to launch a local paper and had already secured some support from an organisation for social entrepreneurs. Their ideas met with an enthusiastic response from Radius, and the *G41* newspaper was born, published by a new social enterprise called Southside Media, which is now constituted as a Community Interest Company. *G41* is sold for 50p a copy. The idea is that if *G41* is successful, it will generate income to be invested in rolling out the model to new areas. Since December 2005, *G41* has been published monthly with 16 pages full of stories and news about local issues and events.

'It's a proper local newspaper and the stories really reflect what is happening in the area. Almost every organisation has a copy and the articles it carries frequently become the topics of conversation. People are clearly more aware of what is going on. It is one of the best things that has happened in the area.' (Local community development worker)

Street representatives

Street representatives are one way of widening the pool of volunteers that has been used in many neighbourhood programmes. For example, St Pauls Unlimited has a pool of 'street ambassadors' – people paid to undertake regular consultation and act as an information source for their street.

Organisational capacity

Organisational and leadership development is a major challenge for Programme participants – facilitators saw it as one of their main areas of work. Much of a community organisation's time is spent responding to immediate demands and bidding for the funds to keep the organisation going, so the capacity for strategic action can be very limited. Even the larger, more professional organisations can be vulnerable when a key player leaves.

Several of the smaller organisations had paid community workers supporting them, while larger organisations had their own staff or employed external consultants to help with organisational issues. However, there are times when community workers themselves cannot offer the support that neighbourhoods need – indeed, several of the original project applications were written by community workers, seeking more support for their local groups. Community workers who were working in Programme neighbourhoods were often isolated and undervalued within their own organisational structures. In at least one case, poor relationships and a lack of commitment from the local authority led to first one worker and then another going on extended sick leave. Paid workers are often trying to cover too many areas – in these circumstances, unless an organisation has obvious problems, they may be happy to just keep a group 'ticking over' and lack the capacity to help it to move forward.

Organisations can, of course, turn to external consultants if they can afford it. However, community organisations do not always have the knowledge, skills and confidence needed to brief and make effective use of a consultant. And the experience of Programme participants suggested that poor services from external consultants may not only waste money but also demoralise the group employing them. On the other hand, Programme facilitators had only limited time and, where the organisation was clear about what was needed, bringing in a consultant to help them review their organisation or to help develop a business plan proved very effective (see the Gellideg example in Box 3.11). In some cases, facilitators helped Programme participants to draft a consultancy brief and make the best use of the consultant appointed.

Matthew Farrell – chair of the Ty Sign Youth Forum – with friends

Leadership is a particularly significant issue for neighbourhood-based organisations and those active within them. Organisational failures, inability to develop and poor partnership development are often blamed on a lack of leadership – and yet few resources are invested in building this capacity. Programme participants have identified a range of characteristics that make for good leadership – including assertiveness; approachability; honesty; charisma and determination – and their experience illustrates how the very process of community involvement in neighbourhood activity can provide an opportunity for both unpaid community members and paid officers to develop their leadership skills, especially where there is access to some mentoring support.

BOX 3.9 THE IMPACT OF COMMUNITY ENGAGEMENT ON INDIVIDUALS

In a number of cases, community involvement has radically changed the way people see and understand the world around them – one person described how he has shifted from being a fairly passive person who found it difficult to strike up a conversation to being much more assertive and with the confidence to speak in a plenary session at a JRF national networking event: "Working with young people has done this ...".

Equally, community engagement can support the development of young people's skills and capacity. One young person has spoken about how he is developing leadership skills of his own: organising events, leading the youth group and representing young people as chair of the council's Youth Forum. Now he is getting other young people involved in the group. "As a young person I've become more mature. I'm seen as a bit of a role model for others now. They treat me like a local councillor sometimes." All this is leading to a change in his career path away from a college course (tourism) towards community work.

Another resident has moved from being an activist lacking in confidence to being a paid worker who is "not scared to speak out". This community participation worker can remember what it is like to be an involved resident but still feel left out of decision making. She is therefore very conscious of the need not to become a gatekeeper of knowledge but a communicator of it: "Now I can see and understand the power issue". Her new role has also opened her eyes to the tensions and dilemmas inherent in her position, including the responsibility of being both a local resident and a locally based paid worker (she could be on call 24 hours a day so she has to be clear about cut-off points). Now that she can go to meetings that she could not access as a resident she realises that a lot of the meetings are not very effective and that "the 'suits' don't know everything"! She also feels that although she carries more clout in some ways, she does not always feel she has the same voice as when she was an activist.

There were also examples within the Programme where the loss of a valued leader had caused difficulties for those left behind, although it has to be said that sometimes a leader moving on can be a benefit, allowing a wider group to take up responsibilities and contacts that had previously been vested in one person. Some of the existing leaders in the Programme had actively encouraged others to get involved and given them the confidence to take up new responsibilities.

A further issue for many organisations arises when they employ people, especially for the first time. There are lots of guidelines to help them recruit, but few to help to manage staff and performance. In addition to the staff management skills required, effective employment practice depends on how much time volunteers are prepared or able to commit, especially where there are difficulties.

BOX 3.10 SOME COMMON EMPLOYMENT CHALLENGES

- Community members take a breather/become less involved after the appointment of paid staff.
- Staffing issues take over a community organisation's agenda and divert it from what it is really about.
- Employment of staff brings a whole set of responsibilities and skills that group members do not necessarily understand, or want to take on (it is not why they got involved).
- There can be a degree of deference and gratitude to the paid worker (especially if they have job titles like 'chief executive' or 'director'), which gets in the way of community leadership and management.
- Tensions often develop between workers and group members in relation to:
  - who represents and 'owns' the group, particularly in dealings with outside bodies such as the council;
  - performance management;
  - who is managing whom, if the community development worker has a role in supporting the development of the management committee.
- Community organisations often have workers imposed on them by larger agencies and therefore feel little control over the service they receive.

On a more positive note, Gellideg Foundation Group offers an excellent example of how staff can be supported.

Colette Watkins of Gellideg Foundation Group in a supervision session with a member of her management team

BOX 3.11 GELLIDEG: EMPOWERING THROUGH SUPERVISION

A major innovation that the **Gellideg Foundation Group (GFG)** introduced in the last year of the Programme was a regular staff review process. This was funded by using JRF credit to buy in the time of a local consultant, who played a strategic deputy role within the organisation, including developing the business plan and sharing the staff reviewing process with GFG's director. The director met monthly with each member of the senior management team, and her new deputy/consultant met with all the other staff for "regular one-to-ones to talk about problems and give support". As a result, staff and volunteer confidence and skills are "much stronger than this time last year". The review process had clear benefits both for the director of the project and for all the project workers. It took the pressure off the project director and allowed her to delegate more tasks. She is now able to stand back from day-to-day issues. The review system also empowered the staff to take more independent decisions and grow and work in new ways that moved them out of their 'comfort zone'. This consultancy arrangement has now ended, but an expansion in staffing has brought in a new Communities First coordinator, who has effectively taken on the deputy manager role.

Working with diversity

Policy makers often speak of the need to develop 'social capital' in communities, on the assumption that community ties are weak. But many communities have strong internal ties already. What they lack is the 'bridging' social capital that builds ties across social groups/communities, both within a neighbourhood and between neighbourhoods. 'Bonding' social capital may help them cope, but it will not help them overcome their problems. Even where individual organisations are quite strong within Programme neighbourhoods, they have often struggled to bring different parts of the community together. The fault-lines may be between different ethnic groups, especially where new groups are seen as a threat by longer-term residents; they may be between generations, with young people being seen as a threat rather than as part of the community. Disabled people, people with mental health problems, travellers or gay, lesbian and transgender people may feel particularly isolated at neighbourhood level.

BOX 3.12 UNDERSTANDING SOCIAL CAPITAL

A common distinction is now made between bonding, bridging and linking social capital.

Bonding social capital describes relationships and networks between people within communities (social glue).

Bridging social capital describes relationships and networks across social groups and communities (social oil).

Linking social capital describes networks and connections between communities and institutions, which cut across status and allow people to exert influence and reach resources outside their normal circles.

Community cohesion is a strong theme in government policy. Creating opportunities for people from different communities to meet together and discover common interests is an essential part of community development. But neighbourhood renewal and other policies can have unintended consequences, with organisations competing with each other for resources and political attention. Wider structural issues can also exacerbate divisions –

An eye-catching mosaic for Full Circle, the Youth and Family Project in St Pauls, Bristol

housing allocations policy is often cited as a cause of resentment. Established organisations with few resources of their own may also be resentful of funding that goes to support new communities, however limited this may be. They may not see why these communities should have separate resources or facilities; they may not recognise that many minorities need support in establishing confidence within their own group before they will be ready to engage more generally.

At the outset of the Neighbourhood Programme, the need to tackle community divisions was identified as a priority for only seven of the 20 neighbourhoods. But we found a variety of creative activities that were building bridges between different organisations at neighbourhood level. The previous section gives examples of the ways in which organisations in the Programme tried to reach out to new or excluded communities within their neighbourhoods, by organising celebratory events and developing 'pioneer' services for new migrants. In addition, groups are organising a range of other opportunities for organisations to come together; building formal partnerships to bridge communities; building equal opportunities into their own practice; and developing protocols to ensure coordination between different organisations.

Opportunities for different organisations to work together

Organisations are setting up specific bridging initiatives, using open spaces or digital technology as a resource.

BOX 3.13 OPPORTUNITIES FOR ORGANISATIONS TO WORK TOGETHER

St Pauls Unlimited has been working with the local authority planning department to reclaim its local park from the drugs trade and improve the environment to foster mixing between members of different communities, especially among women: "Parks provide opportunities for meeting people you wouldn't otherwise meet".

Caia Park Partnership is using digital technology to bring together Polish, Portuguese, Chinese, Czech and other mums and toddlers who are isolated to work on the basics of getting the information they need.

Integrate, Todmorden has put on a number of events to encourage non-Muslims to learn about Islam and has held social events at the mosque, opening the community room in the mosque to people who would not otherwise enter.

Formal partnerships

BOX 3.14 BUILDING BRIDGING ORGANISATIONS

The Broad Street Community Council set up a new group (initially known as 'the JRF Group' because it used Neighbourhood Programme resources) to bring together *dynamo people* from a range of ethnic groups who had an interest in tackling issues such as community safety in the neighbourhood and find common ground with others. This has been successful in attracting BME participants and has also brought in Swindon-wide organisations, such as the Swindon Women's Coalition. It was a member of this group who set up the St Helena Trust mentioned in Box 3.7. The celebratory events described earlier are a major part of their strategy, as is their focus on issues of common concern across ethnic groups in the neighbourhood, such as prostitution and drug dealing.

Getting it sorted: Nazma Ramruttun, John Taylor, Les Horn and Norma Thompson, local activists in Swindon's Broad Street area

Often different groups in a neighbourhood have more in common than they think. The consultation exercise in East Pollokshields allowed people to discover what they had in common and develop an action plan to address it.

BOX 3.15 FINDING COMMON GROUND

In East Pollokshields, the **Southside Housing Association**, as an RSL with an ethnic mix of tenants, appointed a community worker and facilitated a participatory community survey, led by community representatives, which got people from different communities talking to each other. This fed into the development of the **Pollokshields East Partnership**, set up in 2005 to work specifically with diversity and community cohesion issues. It came out of the realisation that there was no agency locally to represent the community as a whole and that the few existing community-wide bodies were predominantly white and not very strong. Yet it was clear that Asian and white residents shared common interests in relation to community safety, as well as play, shopping, community facilities, parking and speeding. The action plan that came out of the survey is well placed to inform the Glasgow-wide Community Planning process.

However, bridging the divide in East Pollokshields has been a slow process:

'It has taken people a very long time to feel comfortable about working together.... It's bloody hard work and we keep having to defend it.'

At the first meeting, the Asian participants would not speak at all, and Asian involvement remains below the 50% level, which is the proportion of Asians in the population. There has been an attempt to set up a rival organisation and the Partnership is still finding it difficult to engage with the mosques or with Asian women.

Out and about on the patch: Southside Housing Association's community worker Smina Akhtar, East Pollokshields

Building equal opportunities into organisational practice

The above examples show the importance of working with individual communities, building informal links and 'bridges' and then institutionalising these links in formal partnerships. It is also important to enshrine good practice on diversity and equalities in neighbourhood organisations themselves.

> ## BOX 3.16 ENSHRINING AND EXTENDING GOOD PRACTICE
>
> **Castle Vale Community Housing Association** has appointed an equalities and diversity coordinator that has given it the capacity to engage a range of groups in partnership work and service delivery. It has also set up a Youth Council, which is providing tasters for engagement with the Neighbourhood Partnership Board and it convenes a practitioner group on young people. It is now seeking to spread this practice into other agencies.

Young people at the launch of the Castle Vale database

Developing agreed ways of working between different local organisations

Where there has been friction between different organisations in a neighbourhood, some kind of agreement about how to coordinate with each other and keep each other informed may be necessary. This was the solution adopted in Caia Park, where there are two major Partnerships both providing services to the neighbourhood. The process of reaching this agreement is discussed in more detail on page 66 and a copy of the agreement can be found in Resource sheet F.

Engaging with power holders

The need for more recognition from power holders was top of the agenda for many organisations in the Programme:

> 'Everything stops at the Town Hall.'

> 'Many authorities don't walk the talk.'

Despite the policy commitment to community engagement, this Programme echoes the findings from too many other initiatives before it: that many community organisations still feel marginalised in partnerships with statutory authorities and agencies. Participants in the

Anyone for a cuppa? Residents at Eastfield, Scarborough, out enjoying the sunshine

Programme claimed that they were frequently ignored by local decision makers and even if they did sit on formal partnerships, partners still took decisions 'over their heads'.

Clearly there is considerable variation between public authorities and several of the organisations reported that relationships had improved during the life of the Programme. The interest that local authorities have in making partnerships work better was evident from the take-up at events held for metropolitan (and unitary) authorities in England and for unitary authorities in Scotland and Wales to share ideas and experience (although perhaps it was significant that an event for county and district councils in England did not attract much interest). Many of those present recognised the advantages for public authorities of community engagement. Four of the applications for organisations to become members of this Programme were written by local authority workers, and several organisations were involved in local authority-led partnerships, were getting community development support from them or had received funding from them.

BOX 3.17 WORKING POSITIVELY WITH POWER HOLDERS I

In **Eastfield,** a good relationship is developing with the local authority, which has expressed an interest in developing neighbourhood management in the area and is holding Neighbourhood Management Strategy Group meetings to plan out what might be feasible; the JRF project has also developed good links with the Learning and Skills Council, through ideas to encourage local recruitment in the nearby Scarborough Business Park.

The business-like approach of the **Boothtown Community Partnership** is met on the council side by a growing willingness to work with (rather than against) local communities. A number of officers who work closely with the Boothtown Community Partnership feel genuinely empowered to do so, although noting that recognition of the benefits of working with communities does not necessarily permeate more traditional 'line departments'. On the council side, the chief executive has sanctioned a Community Engagement Working Group of senior officers to foster joint working with communities – across the 'silos' of local authority departments.

There are also many examples of both interest and positive working in recent publications from both the Improvement and Development Agency (IDeA)[11] and the Local Government Association (LGA).[12]

A joinery workshop supported by Boscombe Working Community Partnership

[11] IDeA (2006)
[12] LGA (2005)

Nonetheless, it is clear from the experience in the Programme that there is still some way to go before community engagement becomes the norm across all public authorities. Even where some officers work closely with the community, engagement depends very much on individual relationships, as the examples in Box 3.17 show. There are positive stories in the Programme of local authorities responding to pressure from local organisations, but it is still far from clear how far 'bottom-up' action in neighbourhoods can change the organisational culture of those local authorities who remain committed to traditional ways of doing things.

While the drive for community engagement from the centre of government has acted as a powerful driver for change in all three countries, other central government policies can get in the way. The pace of policy change puts considerable pressure on relationships between community organisations and their funders or local power holders. Participants remarked on the "danger of policy being confused and the pursuit of policy novelty [being] a bit bewildering". Some areas were grappling with partnership proliferation – several government initiatives within the same neighbourhood competing for local attention and participation – and one project described its early days as a "huge power struggle" for control between the funder, the accountable body and community interests. This underlines the need for a coordinated approach in central government to overcome the problems caused by funding streams controlled by different, sometimes competing departments, each with different boundaries, reporting systems and conditions. Moving – and often narrowing – goalposts were another source of problems. The conditions of SRB funding were described by one project as "a huge bureaucratic nightmare". Programme participants were also critical of the tendency among some power holders to ignore what is already going on the ground and start again from scratch.

Political shifts, personality conflicts and staff turnover all have a major impact on the development of trust and joint working. They can all set back months of progress, but they can also open up new opportunities – a change of council representative in Boscombe made a significant difference to the work of the Partnership and quickly turned a negative relationship into a positive one, while personnel changes at the Regional Development Agency (RDA) have had both positive and negative impacts.

A key variable in the relationship between community organisations and power holders is the political culture of the area – there were considerable differences even within regions. The Programme also reflects experience elsewhere in finding that relationships vary according to service. This varies from neighbourhood to neighbourhood but, while 'clean and green services' and the police tend to be positive, Boothtown found the highways department very resistant to the neighbourhood perspective, while in Pilton the comment was made that the big service departments still tend to go their own way.

BOX 3.18 WORKING POSITIVELY WITH POWER HOLDERS II

Gellideg Foundation Group was persuaded by the local council to take responsibility for the Communities First programme when it was expanded to cover the whole of the ward in which the Foundation operated. It took over from a housing association that had withdrawn from the task. This means that the Group is the fundholder for all the Welsh Assembly's money in the ward. It has also been asked to take over the management of a Healthy Living Centre in another part of Merthyr Tydfil, in recognition of its successful work with a Healthy Living Centre in its own area. However, the group has not been consulted over the housing department's plans for a major development in the area.

Good relationships with the primary care trust in another Programme area were qualified by the complexity of the National Health Service, constant restructuring and the need for health partners to adhere to national objectives. Local economic development agencies have also been difficult to work with – they tend in all three countries to be more concerned with large flagship projects than local economic development. Regional Development Agencies present similar challenges, although the SRB project in Boscombe was able to make important inroads into the economic development agenda at a neighbourhood level (see also the example from Boothtown above).

BOX 3.19 HOW NEIGHBOURHOODS CONTRIBUTE TO ECONOMIC DEVELOPMENT

A major aim of the **Boscombe Working Community Partnership (BWCP)** was to reduce long-term unemployment. The area had a high skill base, but there were no resources for supporting business start-up or self-employment. The partnership worked closely with the borough economic development team, the Prince's Trust, the Chamber of Trade and Business Link Wessex to set up a grants programme for supporting both new and developing business. It awarded £100,000 from its own funds to provide £500 start-up and £1,500 development grants. Support on tap was offered through the Prince's Trust and Business Link. The partnership also contributed capital funding for the development of a new enterprise centre – an incubator facility for new businesses including office space, workshops, training and meeting rooms, which are made available at a considerably reduced rate. Support is also offered when businesses move on. The enterprise centre is consistently full to capacity.

The Boscombe economy seems now to be developing. Two national coffee chains have recently moved into the local shopping precinct, a full-time urban centre manager is in place and the shopping mall is undergoing a mini-refit. To date, over 70 businesses have been supported by BWCP, and this in turn has created over 100 full-time equivalent jobs.

Youth work at Llanharan: 'X factor' entries from Bryncae Youth Club

One of the sticking points for Programme participants was the lack of opportunity to have a strategic voice. Although better services and regeneration projects are important, neighbourhood empowerment requires that neighbourhoods have a voice in strategic planning and policy matters. Even where relationships with local councillors were good, organisations often lacked influence over decisions at authority level.

Smaller organisations in the Programme found it particularly difficult to make an impact in their relationships with the local authority, especially those that were working in pockets of disadvantage within more affluent areas. They were simply not a priority locally and their local authorities rarely had access to regeneration resources. Where such organisations do have resources, they can achieve significant change. They can also act as a useful vehicle to get services into the area and introduce new ideas.

BOX 3.20 YOUTH PROVISION ON A SERVICE LEVEL AGREEMENT: LLANHARAN COMMUNITY DEVELOPMENT PROJECT

In 2002 Rhondda Cynon Taff Council closed its statutory youth club in the village of Bryn Cae, one-and-a-half miles from Llanharan. **Llanharan Community Development Project** was able to open a new youth club under a Service Level Agreement (SLA), in a new venue in September 2004.

This has benefited the young people in that the Llanharan Community Development Project has an experienced staff team and is able to provide a more flexible service. So the young people get a weekly youth club in the holidays as well as in term time, plus a further 16 sessions a year, to allow for attending youth and community events (including the Wales Street Dance Competition). The project is also able to lead skill- and issue-based sessions (eg on sign language) in the computer suite at the Llanharan drop-in centre, and the youth club is brought into community events such as Llanharan village fair.

The SLA also has advantages for the Llanharan Community Development Project. As part of the SLA, the Project has signed up to fulfil six agreed outcomes, but has flexibility in how to do so. This flexibility suits a specialist youth organisation like the Project that has the staff capacity to provide a varied programme. Between 17 and 35 young people attend the club every week – many have been there since the beginning and feel a strong sense of ownership of this community-based youth club.

Local authorities and other agencies hold the power in their relationships with communities and in many ways the onus is on them to change. But there are things that need to change in communities too. Earlier we referred to the need for effective leadership and the failure of some organisations to engage the wider community. Community organisations can very easily lose their credibility with power holders if they are seen to be unrepresentative – one group paid the price of being unwilling to move from the group of six to a group of 26. And, although many of the organisations in the Programme were relentlessly optimistic in their dealings with power holders, there were other cases where too defensive an attitude – attributing negative views of themselves to council officers, always taking an adversarial stance, being unwilling to recognise and acknowledge change – cut off possible lines of negotiation. Organisations may decide that they want to stay outside the system and they will have an important role to play if they do so. But if they do engage, a continually negative stance is not a recipe for building positive relationships.

The relationship with power holders has been a particularly important area of work for the Programme, and later chapters will describe the brokerage role that the Programme has played. Nonetheless, there are examples where organisations have achieved changes on the basis of a solid reputation among partner agencies. This has been the case, for example, in Gellideg (see Box 3.18) and St Pauls in Bristol (see Box 3.21).

Resident activists in a meeting at the St Pauls Unlimited offices

BOX 3.21 WORKING POSITIVELY WITH POWER HOLDERS III

St Pauls Unlimited Community Partnership has built a good reputation with fellow agencies and has achieved significant changes in Bristol City Council's environment and housing policy, particularly in relation to equalities and diversity policies. These include:

- *consultation*: there is now more consultation and a better dialogue, particularly in relation to housing and the environment;
- *planning control*: the planning department works with the community to scrutinise all local planning applications and will oppose those that break up houses into smaller units, in order to ensure the continued availability of housing for families – this approach is now being applied elsewhere in Bristol;
- work to bring *local parks* back into use (see Box 3.13) has also benefited from good relations with the planning department;
- *opportunities to buy*: an innovative scheme to help local people to buy their own homes was pioneered in St Pauls. The RSL now advertises properties for three months in the local community when it is planning to sell them off because they are in poor state of repair. Previously they would have been put on the open market straight away. The council are also looking at shared ownership schemes and other approaches to equity as a way of helping local people increase their stake in local housing.

Sustainability

This Programme has provided a unique opportunity to observe the life cycles of organisations and the ways in which groups ebb and flow. In some cases there has been positive and planned change, for example Castle Vale Housing Action Trust moving on to become Castle Vale Neighbourhood Partnership Board, and Broad Street Community

Council becoming Broadgreen Organisation for Neighbourhood Development. In other cases, organisations have struggled to survive in the face of external pressures. Three of the participating organisations appear to have made little headway during the four years, and four failed to survive in their original form until the end of the Programme. Failure to survive is not always a negative – the Boscombe Working Community Partnership agreed to disband when its SRB funding came to an end as it felt it had done its job and there were other organisations locally supporting community empowerment. In two more cases, the failure of one organisation allowed another to grow. But in two cases there were funding irregularities that were either not spotted or not dealt with by otherwise experienced community leaders. Even organisations that appeared very strong, such as Barne Barton Community Action Trust (later to become Tamar Development Trust) and Norfolk Park Community Forum, experienced difficulties as the Programme progressed. During 2006, both these organisations have gone into financial administration.

Funding

Not surprisingly then, funding and fundraising were identified by most organisations as central concerns. A big theme within action plans is the need to secure and develop community assets as a means of increasing sustainability. Llanharan Community Development Project, for example, has a full-time volunteer specialising in fundraising. Here, every staff member and trustee plays a role in fundraising and income generation and this had paid dividends. However, other organisations have struggled and are caught in a vicious circle – not having the people and skills to raise the funds to bring the people and skills they need into the organisation. Rapid changes in funding programmes and the predominance of limited-term funding streams mean that community organisations face a continual battle to achieve some form of financial sustainability and to manage complex funding packages. Even when a project has done good work, replacing significant funding can be a challenging and time-consuming task, especially where the relationship with the local authority is poor and there is local competition for resources.

New housing on Sheffield's Norfolk Park estate

Several of the larger organisations saw their future in terms of community asset building – some like Castle Vale already had a strong asset base. For others, going down the social enterprise route might seem to be the answer, especially given current government support. But even this was not always the solution. One organisation that was encouraged to become a 'Community Company' wished they had resisted this advice:

'We were expected to do what the private sector can't do – to run a business from scratch which would make a profit AND have community spin-offs.'

BOX 3.22 SOME COMMON FUNDING PROBLEMS

- Neighbourhoods that fall outside priority areas
- Obtaining match funding
- Too many funding streams and lack of coordination between funders
- Lack of skills
- Lack of core funding or funding for pay rises, redundancy, pension provision and so on.
- Cash-flow problems arising from late payment
- Transferring from small grants to the mainstream when special funding disappears

---

The Programme also emphasised the problems that can arise from the absence of effective financial oversight. Where finance is concerned, at least one project found out the hard way that trust is not enough.

Snakes and ladders workshop in full swing at a networking event in Birmingham

Organisational development

But funding is only one part of sustainability. A 'snakes and ladders' exercise at one of the networking days gave us the opportunity to find out what Programme participants saw as key turning points in the lives of their organisations – things that had got in the way of progress (snakes) but also things that had spurred them on (ladders) (see Table 3.1).

Table 3.1 Life cycle turning points (snakes and ladders)

'Ladders'	'Snakes'
The appointment of a worker	Increase in staff creates increased management
A community fun day leads to setting up a residents association	Leading volunteer dies
Community elections give power to local representatives	
Survey helps raise interest and gives useful community information	
Moved into own community building	Move of community facility damages sense of community and local services
Change in council policy improves local opportunities	Significant change in funding criteria
	New Community Planning Partnership left group powerless
Decent Homes Standard in place	Long delays in building programme – had an active community until demolition started
	Stock transfer ballot – housing regeneration stopped!

It was encouraging to find that participants identified more positive turning points than negative ones but what quickly become clear (and is illustrated in Table 3.1) is that the same turning point can be both positive and negative depending on the circumstances. For example, the appointment of a community worker was positive for some organisations but not for others; the election of a new chairperson brought success for some organisations and disaster for others; partnership development was a source of opportunity for some, but imposed restrictions on others. There is no one model for successful organisational development. Even within one organisation, a particular development might have both 'pros' and 'cons'. For example, while the setting up of more professional systems to manage staff and money may be seen as positive, it can also distract community members from their original purpose and isolate them from the wider community. In other words, ladders – for example, funding for a staff team – can become snakes – for example, "management problems slow us down". On the other hand, apparent crises can become new opportunities. For example, a key person leaving can be a disaster but it can encourage others to take on more responsibility.

The Programme also demonstrated the impact that external policies and programmes have on community organisations. Most organisations see the current emphasis on 'neighbourhoods' and the regeneration and housing agenda as positive. But at the same time, these can cause new and unanticipated difficulties for Programme participants: delivery agencies falling out with each other; new partnerships imposed on top of existing neighbourhood-based organisations; stock transfer undermining development; and demolition stripping the heart out of the community.

Will it go in? Wrexham's Caia Park Tenancy Support Team moving furniture

4

The JRF Neighbourhood Programme: how it worked

In Chapter 3 we identified a number of problems and issues that organisations in the Programme's neighbourhoods faced. Table 4.1 shows how they used the various Programme resources to address these.

Table 4.1 How JRF helped

Barriers to empowerment	How JRF helped
Analysis: no coherent analysis of local problems and assets	Action planning and review
Engagement: people not engaged, little activity going on locally to tackle problems	Exchanging knowledge through: JRF materials; facilitators; networking and visits; joint project
Capacity: lack of leadership; lack of organisational capacity; low level of skills; low level of resources	Credit; knowledge exchange as above; facilitator offering training, mentoring and support
Cohesion: community is divided and fragmented Local groups are not working effectively together	Exchanging knowledge through networking, visits and joint project; brokerage and facilitation
Power and influence: power holders ignore the community; policy is not geared to local need	Kitemarking by JRF; exchanging knowledge through networking and visits; brokerage and facilitation; knowledge generation through thematic research (joint project)
Sustainability: future uncertain, no sustainable funding	Brokerage; joint project on funding
National recognition and policy support: need for policy framework that supports empowerment and help to break down barriers	Dissemination; local authority events; policy influence

Action planning

We saw in Chapter 2 that to start with many organisations were resistant to action planning. However, as the Programme progressed and participants were encouraged to use the plan for annual review, smaller organisations, in particular, began to see the value of this approach.

BOX 4.1 THE IMPORTANCE OF ACTION PLANNING

For one small group, action planning meant that members had to "share ideas" and "discuss how their work was developing". Without an action plan, they "wouldn't have had anything to judge progress":

> 'Only when you reflect on it do you realise what you have achieved.'

Another group said that it "sets your sights on something". They planned to continue using the action planning process after the end of the Programme.

How action planning was used

The format for the action plan review process can be found in Resource sheet D. As the comments from participants show, this process served a number of useful purposes. It provided space for reflection away from the day-to-day pressures of delivering services. It also provided a benchmark. A particularly popular aspect of the review process was asking the group to score progress on each aim and objective in the plan either using numbers or a traffic light system, which allowed them to recognise and validate their progress. Most organisations found that this was the only opportunity they had to feel proud of their work and pat themselves on the back for their ceaseless effort. For smaller organisations especially, an additional benefit was to ensure that the whole group was involved in discussions of their aims and progress rather than just one or two people.

Action planning needn't be boring! Leanne Roach, Sam Dunbar and Carol Blackburn from Plymouth's Tamar Development Trust

Facilitation

Two years into the Programme, organisations were asked which of the different resources they found most useful. The chart in Figure 4.1, which shows the percentage selecting each type of resource, demonstrates that, at this time, organisations found the facilitation resource far and away the most useful and the website the least useful.

Figure 4.1 Relative value placed on JRF resources by neighbourhoods (2004)

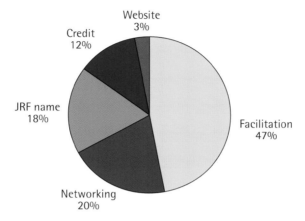

A further two years on, facilitation is still rated very highly. The ongoing commitment of up to 30 days' facilitation over three years that the Programme provided is a resource that few community organisations outside the Programme have access to. The fact that there is a continuous relationship with one facilitator and is reinforced by their presence at networking events allows for the development of trust over time.

The JRF Programme provided a facilitator to work with all participating organisations. One facilitator was selected by the Foundation for each country/region, and all facilitators were highly experienced – also bringing status and credibility with external agencies. As they

Talking regeneration – Scotland facilitator Michael Carley in discussion with Pilton Partnership's Ian Cooke

worked with many other projects and programmes outside JRF, they brought a national perspective. However, being 'of the region', they also brought a regional understanding.

How facilitators were used

The role of the facilitators was defined by JRF as one of experts who were 'on tap, not on top', available to help the neighbourhood organisations to define their aims and to carry them out, but not to define issues for the neighbourhoods. The organisations were to use the facilitators as they saw fit – for example, as mentor to the group leader or worker, to give technical advice, to facilitate events on team building or strategic business planning and so on.

Table 4.2 summarises the views of the facilitators and the organisations in the Programme on what the facilitators were able to offer.

Table 4.2 Roles undertaken by facilitators

What the facilitators say	What the organisations say
Confidence building Listening ear Bearing witness 'Modelling' behaviour	"... comes to most of our monthly meetings, worked on our business plan, lettings policy; she knows so many people in the area and has given us confidence. ..." "provided secretarial support to the Community Centre steering group. ..."
Planting seeds Asking the interesting/difficult/lateral questions Sharing judgement Reminding people to keep things on agenda	"Support, information sharing and information gathering, brokerage and generally just being available to bounce ideas and issues off. ..." "Keeping focus."
Critical friend, mentoring	"[Provides] constructive advice and criticism. ..." "... has been mentoring our coordinator. ..." "... [staff] issues arising from organisational development and future planning. ..."
Someone to turn to ... (sometimes) in a crisis	"... steering us when we needed help. ..." "... signposted us to who to approach to get things done. ..."
Helping groups to think strategically Broadening horizons	
Go-between, mediator, opening doors to power holders (brokerage)	"... explaining how the council works. ..."

Forging a trusting relationship was crucial – and having access to the same person over several years was crucial to building trust.

The facilitation role in the Programme was significantly different from 'consultancy'. One organisation commented: "He is not a consultant – the facilitator role is more active and closer to the action. It is a more measured approach." While all the facilitators had consultancy experience, consultants are usually called in by a client to do a particular job, where the client knows what they want from the consultant and there is a very specific role. Or they are called in to solve a specific problem. In the Neighbourhood Programme, the role of the facilitator was less specific or problem-oriented. This allowed for far more flexibility, but it caused some difficulties to start with. One facilitator commented: "I don't know what product I am selling". In some cases, the action planning process (see page 50) helped facilitators to establish a role and relationship, but in other cases, it took much longer to form relationships and clarify expectations. Some organisations hardly used their facilitators at all in the first year, in part because they did not know how to make best use of them.

Diagnosis was a key element of the facilitation role. The facilitators found that "the 'presenting problem' is not always the 'real problem'" – indeed some took the view that moving from the presenting problem offered by the organisation to the 'nub' of the real problem was a key task for a facilitator. Another fundamental role for facilitators was to 'broaden their horizons' – to contribute towards problem definition and not just work towards solutions for problems already clearly identified by the organisations. Both tasks require a subtle and sophisticated approach and are dependent on both trust and familiarity with the local situation.

As the Programme progressed, facilitators found themselves taking on more of a *mentoring* role: someone trustworthy at the end of a phone who could stand above the local politics, "without an axe to grind". This mentoring role was normally with a key community group member, but it could be equally important for an isolated community worker. It was important, however, to ensure that a good one-to-one relationship did not prevent contact between the Programme and other staff or group members. The relationship between the Programme and the participating organisation could not afford to be too dependent on one person. Sometimes, facilitators were also able to help address staff management issues, although this could be tricky and, in one case, led to a distinct cooling of the relationship between the facilitator and the project. Facilitators also played an important role in *brokerage* – a role to which we return on page 62.

Identifying the right role to play, with limited days available, requires skills and experience, and the approach taken by facilitators varied, in part because of the differing needs and context of the organisations and in part because of their own different strengths, expertise and style: "All [of us] facilitators have worked in different ways with different groups, but to our strengths". All the facilitators saw the value of actively *doing* some of the tasks associated with community organisation where necessary, for example taking notes at meetings or managing planning meetings for an event. For some of the smaller organisations, this could help to move things forward and to 'model' ways of working and organising – as one facilitator said: "Sometimes it is necessary 'to do' as well as to enable". But it was important to get the balance right and to know when to be "a bit pushy" and when to stand back – it was "important that this happens as a result of careful judging about when to intervene with particular kinds of help". It was also important to ensure that this was only a temporary role and one that organisations took over for themselves. Ultimately, as one of the facilitators said: "This model is about building supportive tissue. ... limited but tenacious light touch support".

The impact of facilitation

Participants' assessments of the JRF neighbourhood facilitators were overwhelmingly positive (see Box 4.2).

Jenny Lynn – the Yorkshire facilitator – with Gary Lofthouse, Iris O'Donnell and Jayne Lofthouse from the Boothtown Community Partnership in Halifax

BOX 4.2 THE POSITIVE VALUE OF THE FACILITATION ROLE

'[The facilitator's] support has been excellent both for our organisation and for me personally. ...

'The organisation is more open and democratic with a shiny new code of practice for trustees and a new memorandum and articles and three more board members. ... The Partnership has more respect from our partner agencies.'

'The facilitation role led to confidence building. This constant push – her knowledge, constant positivity from outside person – provides a buzz. She's objective – no hidden agenda, she shares everything ... she has played a crucial role on many levels.'

Having the *support* of a JRF facilitator "at the end of the phone" was for many organisations a great help in making them feel calm and capable. They felt comfortable in the relationship and able to ask any question and get advice. Having this ongoing support helped to provide continuity for the organisations when key local allies – for example, within the local authority – moved on.

At the minimum, facilitation helped organisations to 'stop rolling back down the hill'. It often achieved much more – many organisations felt they had moved on, developing an increased understanding of the barriers they faced and the wider context. But facilitation is not the panacea for all ills, and not all organisations could identify such a positive impact. Facilitators' styles varied, and whereas some organisations would have preferred a more directive approach, there were others who felt that their facilitator had been too intrusive, raising issues in a way that they found unhelpful. And while most appreciated the access that a well-connected facilitator could open up to more powerful stakeholders, there were organisations who would have preferred to have been taken seriously on their own merit.

One of the several murals that add a splash of colour to life in St Pauls, Bristol

How to make the most of facilitation

This leads to the following observations about how and when facilitation works best.

Time

This report has stressed the importance of having time to build up a trusting relationship. Facilitators suggested that in order to make the process work as effectively as possible, eight to 10 days a year would probably be the minimum (allowing a visit every four to six weeks).

There were also criticisms of the amount of facilitation available. Organisations were allocated a fixed amount of facilitation time – for some, the fixed amount of time available (15 or 30 days over three years) was not enough, while others did not use their full allocation. Some participants thought that facilitation time should have been reviewed and possibly pooled so that help and support could be provided in the most appropriate way and at the most appropriate time.

The right match

While the regional distribution had a lot to recommend it in terms of local knowledge, there were some questions about whether the Programme had achieved the right match between facilitators and organisations, given the range of skills and approaches on offer. There was also a suggestion that JRF could have given more attention to developing relationships between facilitators and organisations at the beginning of the Programme, perhaps at a networking event, which would have allowed facilitator and neighbourhood participants to be matched rather than being "thrown together".

Clarity

While the flexibility of the role has generally been an asset, some took the view that the action planning process could have been used to establish a clearer contract with the facilitator. Indeed, with the benefit of hindsight, a launch meeting of the whole network at the outset would have provided an opportunity to give organisations an identity with the Programme, to introduce facilitators and to explain how the Programme would work.

Credit

A second significant Programme resource was the provision of a small sum of money that the group could spend as it wished at any time during the life of the Programme. Credit decisions were largely based on the extent to which organisations already had resources available to them. Out of the 20 organisations in the Programme, 10 organisations were allocated a credit line of £10,000 spread over the three years of the Programme, six organisations were allocated £5,000 and four – which already had significant funding – none, although one of these organisations traded credit for extra facilitation time. All of the organisations that were awarded credit received cheques for their first (or only) £5,000 up front; those qualifying for £10,000 could claim their second amount once the first £5,000 had been accounted for.

How credit was used

Organisations were generally given a free rein in terms of how and when they used their credit. It supported a wide variety of activities, examples of which are shown in Table 4.3.

The Broad Street neighbourhood in Swindon

Table 4.3 Using credit

Joint local events, parties, room hire and refreshments, festival equipment, toys	"It helped to fund a project to take kids off the street in the summer and teach them worthwhile skills both on computer and in taking part in games, painting, etc." "It helped to make it the biggest Eid celebration we have organised."
Regeneration magazines and newsletters, software for bilingual newsletter, marketing/publicity	
Training packages, travel to JRF national/regional events, childcare	"We plan to give some financial support to help one of our members gain youth work qualifications." "We spent it on an accredited training course on management for our coordinators."
Equipment: a laptop, projector, digital camera	
Consultation/advice, eg professional fees to an architect and lawyer	"We put the rest towards bringing in Mentor [an organisation providing professional personnel support]."
Match funding for the production of the Community Profile	
A planning application for a community building, shutters for a community shop	"We could not have got the shutters without the credit, without the shutters could not have got the shop, without the shop nothing would have happened."

For some of the smaller organisations, this credit was their first funding, and often represented as large an amount of money as they felt they could comfortably manage. Some of them were able to identify clear purposes for the money and used it straight away. In others, credit was reserved for a 'rainy day':

'It was very important in setting up our activities. This is the first funding that we have received as a group. It has been good to have some over to allocate to future plans.'

'It's very important to know there is that money there, waiting for our use when our organisation needs it.'

In larger organisations (with lower allocations) the money often went unspent initially, partly due to the difficulty of earmarking specific uses for this small amount of money in the wider, more complex financial flows that these organisations were managing. In the later stages of the Programme, however, these larger organisations became more creative in spending credit: hiring consultants for specific training packages and other support services, for example. And in the few cases where organisations were not making use of credit, facilitators were often able to spot potential opportunities to do so as they became familiar with the organisation's work. While the pace of credit spending was slow to pick up, therefore, most organisations felt they had made good use of it in the end and valued the flexibility in how and when they were allowed to spend it.

As with facilitation, there was some criticism of the allocations and some Programme participants suggested that these should have been reviewed (although such a review did result in one organisation giving up its credit for extra facilitation). Having no credit could "reinforce a sense of powerlessness". Even where a project is in receipt of major funding, there are often conditions to this funding and a small amount of 'free' money can be surprisingly effective.

The impact of credit

The value of small amounts of money with few strings attached has been demonstrated elsewhere.[13] One of the facilitators commented that it demonstrated the shortcomings of so much, more regulated, funding practice:

> 'The groups have used credit with only the smallest amount of control, very largely to good effect and often with remarkable ingenuity and significant visible impact, contrary to what some people might have expected in such a relaxed funding regime.'

Networking

The Programme was conceived as a learning network (see Chapter 2). Programme participants came together with facilitators, the JRF team and the evaluation team for a series of two-day national networking events. These networking events were probably the point at which Programme participants felt closest to the JRF Programme and part of a 'whole'. Two events were held in each year – one at a weekend and one in the week to maximise the opportunity to attend. Evaluations at each meeting informed the design of later meetings. Although most of the meeting was devoted to giving participants the opportunity to share their own experience, outside speakers were also brought in so that participants could hear about good ideas from elsewhere. Some Programme participants also went to the annual National Regeneration Convention, of which JRF is a joint organiser, as speakers and/or participants.

Networking events helped to put the work in each neighbourhood in a wider context and demystify the wider world of regeneration. They also presented an opportunity for UK-wide learning. To begin with, some participants questioned the relevance of a national network to their immediate concerns. Two of the Welsh organisations, for example, suggested that the difference between national funding streams and policies between countries meant there was little value in networking with English organisations. However, their view changed over time and participants generally found cross-border links useful. A Scottish group who "made contact with a couple of others from English neighbourhoods after meeting them at national networking event" found that non-Scottish neighbourhood organisations gave them a valuable outside perspective.

There were also regional meetings, with organisations from Wales and the South West holding joint meetings in the latter half of the Programme, despite the reservations reported above.

---

[13] ODPM (2005)

Delegates enjoying a workshop at one of the national networking events

'The networking events were excellent. Initially it was just the Welsh groups meeting which was really good, but when we joined together with the West Country groups it was excellent. These gave the opportunity for visits to other projects, something that just would not have happened without JRF.'

These were found to be useful for the following reasons: discussing practical issues, problems and solutions; networking; sharing good practice and information. The regional meetings also acted as inter-project visits, allowing others in the region to see what the host group had achieved. In Wales, in particular, the regional meetings have encouraged more informal links between Programme participants around mutual help and advice on funding.

BOX 4.3 NETWORKING IN WALES

People from **Llanharan** have attended both the national JRF networking events and regional events for Wales and the South West. This has allowed them to pick up useful ideas, for example through a workshop on anti-social behaviour orders at one of the regional events. Within Wales stronger links have developed, leading to some contact outside the events: "I have no qualms about phoning her"; "Caia, too, ... been very happy to share information about funding."

How networking events were used

A good experience of the networking events was critical to feeling part of the Programme as a whole. But Programme participants used the opportunity in different ways. Some organisations felt that there was a value in sending different people each time to spread the benefits of participation. However, while it is empowering to spread the opportunity to network as widely as possible, there is also a value in having people at the event who know the Programme and can share their experience. This also helps to build coherence between the networking event and other aspects of the Programme. When key people from a participating organisation did not attend, this undermined the link between the group and the Programme as a whole (as would be the case in any partnership or network). One organisation had a policy of keeping one representative throughout while changing the other each time and this might be the most effective compromise – maintaining continuity while also broadening the personal links and learning that the networking events provided.

Some organisations attended fewer network meetings than others. The Joseph Rowntree Foundation acknowledged the difficulty that some people might have in giving up their time given other pressures in their lives. However, there was a feeling that attendance should have been part of the 'contract' with JRF, and that these Programme participants benefited far less from the Programme than the others. Indeed, two of the larger organisations that otherwise made little use of the Programme always sent people to the networking meetings, who were active participants and gave positive feedback on the experience.

However much people valued national and regional networking meetings, it was difficult to get Programme participants to go to any further meetings and even the regional meetings were patchy in attendance. Organising further meetings for the Programme's 'joint projects' proved impossible:

> 'Getting people out of their environment is very difficult … people have enough trouble coordinating their own projects, let alone meeting up with others.'

However, as we have seen, networking events did lead in some cases to organisations arranging visits to each other outside the formal processes of the Programme.

A workshop at a Wales/South West regional networking event

The impact of networking

The networking events were the second most popular resource in the Programme. Both group members and support workers valued the opportunity to meet others who faced similar issues and problems:

> 'We started off really nervous, but built confidence and made friends at the networking events and the convention too.'

> 'When we first came to a Networking Event we were petrified. Two years later we will go anywhere. We have the confidence.'

There has been a buzz at these events and the event evaluations have been very positive. Initial fears people had about whether they would look right – "what to wear" – and how to behave, were quickly quelled. People from other neighbourhoods appeared to be "down to earth". The informality of the events helped: "A five-minute conversation while queuing for coffee can be very productive!". Group members felt their expertise was taken seriously, even by "the academics". Some realised that they were "not a minnow", but a bigger player than they realised. The events also gave participants a space where they did not have to watch their backs: "At JRF you could speak as you felt, not like neighbourhood politics".

The events allowed participants to discover, value and share what they know, providing mutual learning and support. They felt that it was important to "know we are not alone", and were inspired by ideas and inputs from speakers and workshop presenters, as well as from other participants. Attending networking events gave organisations the opportunity to find out what others were doing and "what problems they have". Participants felt that these events set their experience in a wider context of common problems and potential solutions. Indeed, one of the less obvious benefits was that listening to the problems of other organisations can also lead to a feeling of "oh, at least we've got that one cracked!".

BOX 4.4 THE VALUE OF NETWORKING

'The networking has been invaluable, both as an opportunity to share information and good practice, share problems and challenges – but just being with other like-minded people is refreshing and invigorating and enthuses you – the importance of this should not be underestimated.' (Member of one of the larger organisations)

'Networking/regional conferences have been the highlight. I cannot emphasise the importance enough of allowing us all to get together to learn and share and feel our message is getting across to those who influence decisions.'

Information and knowledge

One of the rationales for setting up the Programme was to share the knowledge that the Foundation had acquired through its research over the years. At the outset the Programme manager signposted Programme participants to relevant JRF *Findings*, and these were also available at networking meetings. Although organisations made little reference to these when asked about their use of Programme resources, they did have their enthusiasts: "I was a big fan already (from my previous job) especially of the *Findings* which are excellent, concise and can let you know if it is worth reading more". Both the Programme manager and facilitators kept participants up to date with information relating to their work, and many organisations found email and telephone contact with the Programme manager extremely useful.

The website set up for the Programme was not a great success, however, and was not widely used. Participants who had accessed the site were generally positive, and had found it "a good source of info on events and funding opportunities". They had used it for specific queries, to get information on JRF publications, "to identify and review research" or to find out what other Programme participants were doing: '[We accessed it] for a query regarding an accounting package, for which we received useful feedback". In one case the local community development worker scanned the site and found it useful to find out what other organisations are up to across the Programme.

But there were access problems. Not all of the Programme participants had internet access. Several who had tried to access the site had found it a struggle; one had "failed miserably" and then "gave up trying". Others said that they did not know how to access it. One confessed to the fact that theirs was "not a terribly computer-literate project".

Some also questioned the wisdom of setting up a website in the first place:

> 'It is a good idea but it takes time to establish and I feel there is such a lot out there on the web anyway.'

Why was the website not a success? After all, received wisdom suggests that communications technology has the potential to transform the way that communities can operate. One reason may be technical – that this site was difficult to access and negotiate; another might be that with so many websites available, any new one has to offer added value – something distinctive. But comments from participants also suggested that many organisations may not have the confidence or resources to engage with this technology. Greater confidence in this respect could help Programme participants in their aspirations to involve young people more effectively, but it is clear that the internet is not a panacea. Indeed, this experience has been repeated in a major national programme – the Children's Fund – which found that people used email to network and share information instead.[14]

Brokerage

Chapter 3 demonstrates how difficult relationships can be both within communities and between them and power holders. As the Programme developed, the potential for the Foundation to act as an 'honest broker' when difficulties arose became more and more apparent.

How brokerage was used

There were a number of situations that triggered a brokerage intervention:

- In one case, the local authority gave very short notice for the withdrawal of very substantial amounts of Neighbourhood Renewal funding, without observing due process.
- In another, the local authority responded to a new national programme by setting up a completely new partnership, despite the existence of a community-based partnership in the area already.
- Another organisation in the Programme was operating alongside two other government-funded initiatives but, although there was no conflict, there was little positive contact between them. This organisation was also experiencing difficulties with its funder, the RDA.

---

[14] Edwards et al (2006)

Agencies in Caia Park sign the protocol for joint working

- In a fourth organisation, past difficulties appeared to be impeding effective collaboration between the local authority, developers, the community and other agencies in a local regeneration programme.

In the second and third examples above, the facilitator acted as broker, while in the first and fourth, JRF staff and the Programme chair were brought in to use their 'clout' to press for change. Nonetheless, facilitators who engaged in brokering processes were clearly seen by both Programme participants and other stakeholders in the area as representing JRF and therefore brought the JRF reputation with them even where Foundation players were not involved:

> 'We would have had extreme difficulty ourselves and needed an outside organisation [to make the process of developing a code of conduct work]. Our facilitator, as outsider, could make everyone look at what was going on more and he brought honesty to the proceedings.'

BOX 4.5 THE VALUE OF BROKERAGE

In **Caia Park,** the sometimes uneasy relationship between the Caia Park Partnership and the new Communities First Partnership led to a series of meetings between the main community agencies in the area. The facilitator prepared for these by sounding out partners in advance and preparing a report on their views. The three agencies agreed to hold a wider meeting of local groups to talk about the feasibility of setting up a development trust for Caia Park, in which they would all have a stake. They also drew up an agreed protocol for joint working (which can be found in Resource sheet F). Among other things, this protocol ensured that the partners signing up to the protocol would consult on any new initiative that was likely to have an impact on each other. In time the precise clauses of the protocol become largely irrelevant – it was the process of negotiating and working together that was most important.

Being able to bring the JRF name to bear was of great benefit in getting more powerful stakeholders and advisors to the table. Where action was needed at a very senior level, it paid to be able to field national figures. It ensured that key players sat up and took notice. Having a high profile champion also made the project feel less alone and gave it more options, especially in a crisis situation. But there was one occasion when attempts to meet with the chief executive in one authority failed, despite the fact that she had attended one of the Programme's local authority events (see below), and in another case, views differ as to how successful the process was.

Brokerage is not the answer to everything. Difficulties remain in all of the examples described here. It is, in any case, difficult to define success – mediation is seldom a 'quick fix' and both external and internal forces can upset a fragile truce. This makes it even more important that organisations can call on someone they know and have a trusted relationship with.

Brokerage also requires some difficult balancing acts. Finding the right approach and the appropriate circumstances can be a very subtle process, with a need to check out constantly the views of the different stakeholders and the approach being used.

Learning from brokerage

Preparation

Where high-level intervention was required, it was still important to lay the ground properly. Brokerage was a team effort and the behind-the-scenes work of facilitators in sounding people out and putting a range of views on the table was extremely important. It was also important to prepare the local project or group to take a full and constructive part.

BOX 4.6 THE IMPORTANCE OF PREPARATION

In **Boscombe** the local SRB project had a difficult relationship with its funding RDA. A change of personnel at the RDA offered the promise of better relationships, but when the new link officer left after a few months, the uncertainty returned. Although the project had good relations with senior personnel, the project got mixed messages about the conditions of its funding and was often left 'guessing what the rules were' as requirements changed. Link officers rarely had an understanding of the voluntary sector. When the periodic funding review meeting was held, the facilitator worked with the partnership to help them to recognise their achievements and focus on the positives. They went into the meeting feeling very confident. The link person from the RDA at this meeting was also very positive and honest about the difficulties. When the issue of administrative support was raised the local authority representative who was present agreed to pick up the bill, and the outcome of the meeting was much more positive than anyone anticipated.

Follow-up

Clarity at the end of the meeting on what will happen next is also important, as are opportunities for the local group or groups to get together and 'debrief'. In one case, brokerage did not work because, despite the fact that an initial meeting gave the project a "fair wind, with agencies wanting to work constructively with the Forum in the future", there was not a sufficient follow-up to the meeting and the momentum was lost.

Time

Conflict resolution is a process that requires ongoing support and relationship building between the parties concerned – relationships often get worse before eventually settling down. For example, in the case of the project that faced the threat of its Neighbourhood

Joan Hubbard (foreground) of Norfolk Park Community Forum, another organisation that asked JRF for brokerage services

Renewal funding being withdrawn, legal action was threatened. This was successful in averting the funding crisis but, not surprisingly, it did not improve relationships. However, a third meeting, once the situation had cooled down, was much more "friendly and helpful" and gave an opportunity both for the council to explain changes in Neighbourhood Renewal funding and for the development trust to outline its own future plans.

Keeping the group centre stage

Finally, while JRF was a useful ally to have on board, it was important to ensure that high profile meetings did not draw attention away from the local organisation itself. This could paradoxically weaken the organisation in the longer term, if it felt marginalised or if others felt it could not make its own case. Local players might also resent a small local organisation bringing in national players (although we did not have evidence of this in the Programme). It is also important to ensure that the discussion is not hijacked by wider policy issues, rather than focusing on the needs of the particular group.

Kitemarking: the value of the JRF brand

The validation that the JRF name offers has been extremely important in raising the profile of local groups and has been highly valued, especially by smaller community-led organisations and those experiencing difficulty in their relationships with more powerful local actors:

> 'Not counting the facilitation, the most important was the name and presence of JRF in our corner.'

Vicky Robertshaw (centre) of the Boothtown Community Partnership in Halifax, who found she could use the JRF name to good effect

Programme participants confessed that they had used it "constantly" and "relentlessly":

'We name drop all the time.... It is quite prestigious to be part of the Programme.'

'Yes, we use it constantly – at every public event and in every funding application.'

They used the JRF name for publicity and to gain recognition from local power holders and other local agencies. Examples include the launch event for East Pollokshields Community Plan and two events in Eastfield, one hosted by Lord Best, where JRF attracted in a range of stakeholders. In the latter case, the local group felt that the JRF association had put the neighbourhood on the radar of the local authority and moved it from being "nowhere" to being considered seriously as the place to pilot neighbourhood management.

BOX 4.7 IMPACT OF THE JRF NAME

The JRF name confers a feeling of credibility, especially when talking to outside organisations:

'The JRF name carries much respect and we have used it on several occasions to influence decisions.'

'JRF is the magic word around here. Amazing! Quite early on mentioned JRF in a meeting with Landfill Tax Credit people and heads shot up.'

Membership of the Programme has also been used in funding applications:

'The name JRF has been more important than the money as we have used that in a lot of bids that we have put in for funding different projects.'

A national platform: Bringing 'Neighbourhood' Centre Stage

As part of the Neighbourhood Programme three events under the banner of Bringing 'Neighbourhood' Centre Stage were held for local authority chief executives, leaders and other senior staff. In Scotland and Wales, other public and community organisations also attended. These provided an opportunity for local authorities and others to explore the role for neighbourhoods in local governance and the links between neighbourhood regeneration and service delivery. All were attended by the Foundation's director, JRF staff and trustees, as well as some practitioners from the Neighbourhood Programme.

The English and Scottish events were 24-hour events and the reports of the events were circulated to a broader range of local authorities and other agencies. Twenty-nine local authorities were represented across the three events along with a range of partner agencies. The Foundation also organised meetings with civil servants in key government departments in all three countries to share emerging findings.

If the neighbourhood agenda is to be effective, it needs to be part of the culture of local authorities and other public bodies. These JRF events were an opportunity to promote discussion between senior local and national government personnel and gain commitment. Particularly valuable were the 24-hour events with the Chatham House Rule[15] that allowed senior local authority staff to respond honestly to the challenges that JRF raised. One-off events, however inspirational, have their limitations. As one such meeting emphasised, learning happens by doing and by a continuous exposure to the value of a neighbourhood approach. But the events did provide an opportunity for the experience and learning from the Neighbourhood Programme to be shared with some key policy implementors, although there was only very limited direct involvement of neighbourhood organisations themselves in the events. It also provided opportunities to present interesting practice from outside the Programme, particularly from local authorities themselves, and to share learning across countries. A summary of the main points raised can be found in Appendix 3.

---

[15] The Chatham House Rule governs the confidentiality of the source of information at a meeting.

5

Working effectively in neighbourhoods

'For me the innovative aspect of the programme was ... the support that JRF gave to community organisations and how that support enabled them to make more effective contributions within their neighbourhoods. Everyone knows that community organisations are central to neighbourhood renewal but how they contribute and what support they need to do it effectively and sustainability never seems to get much attention. The perceived wisdom is that you throw a few short-term grants at groups and they'll somehow make it all work. I think this programme demonstrates an effective, value-for-money way that trusts and local authorities could replicate to support neighbourhood organisations.' (Advisory group member)

The Joseph Rowntree Foundation Neighbourhood Programme has now run its course. The evidence that we have from participants suggests that many individuals and organisations feel that their membership of the Programme has benefited them. Their ability to self-organise is significantly greater. Key individuals have developed a community leadership role. The association with JRF has significantly boosted their confidence and in some cases the status of their organisations. It seems likely that this confidence has contributed to their capacity to deal with adversity, to develop innovative ideas, to be ambitious and to make progress.

Returning to the stages of development, discussed in Chapter 2, Table 5.1 shows where Programme participants were by the end of the Programme.

Table 5.1 Neighbourhood organisations by stage of development

		Programme start	Programme end
Stage 1	Just starting out as community groups	8 organisations	3 organisations
Stage 2	Service delivery organisations, engaging with potential partners	4 organisations	2 organisations
Stage 3	Beginning to take strategic leadership role in the neighbourhood	4 organisations	6 organisations
Stage 4	Mature organisations who could share experience and with interest in national profile	4 organisations	6 organisations
Closure	Group folded		3 organisations*

Note: *In a fourth area, the organisation that folded was replaced by a new group, with the support of the Programme.

An aerial shot of a regenerated Castle Vale. The work was carried out by Castle Vale Housing Action Trust, certainly the best funded organisation in the JRF Programme

As the table shows, this light touch support has not worked for everyone. While some of the organisations, and the people within them, have grown and become much stronger, a few have made little headway. For some of the smallest and most fragile organisations, the JRF 'light touch' was too light – they would have needed a more intensive intervention to make any significant advance. Similarly, with the largest organisations it was difficult to see what the Programme could offer that would make a significant difference to them (although two of them were assiduous attendees at networking events and gave positive feedback on these). Experience suggests, therefore, that there may be a threshold of capacity and resources below which it is difficult for organisations to benefit from this kind of light touch support, and a ceiling above which it gives little added value.

Other factors affecting the impact of the Programme cut across size. First, it was important that there was a 'champion' in the group or the neighbourhood who remained committed to working with the Programme throughout. The way the Programme was set up, through organisations being nominated by a third party, created some problems with 'buy-in'. It meant that some organisations were never really clear why they were in the Programme and how they could best use it. Second, the relationship with the facilitator was important. In a couple of cases, the match between facilitator and project did not work out. Conversely, those organisations who already knew and had a relationship with their facilitator were able to achieve a great deal, whatever their size.

As with most other neighbourhood interventions, it took time for the Programme to develop. After two years, there was a not a great deal to show in terms of added value. However, this has changed over the second two years, with the benefits becoming more evident. How sustainable these benefits are, it is difficult to predict. Individuals move on within both organisations and partner agencies, and it is not always clear how far within organisations the support of the Programme has penetrated. However, the benefits are likely to be carried into other places by those who do move on.

We have already reported that, despite the best efforts of the Programme, four organisations failed to survive to the end of the Programme in their original form, and one more will close shortly. The particular circumstances of these failures raise questions about the capacity of even experienced organisations to manage staff or to ensure transparency in funding. However, their closure does not necessarily constitute Programme failure. In one case, the Programme identified an alternative organisation to work with in the same neighbourhood and this has now become a strong group with recognition from the local authority. In two more, there has been evidence of learning in the community or among the power holders, which may well be sustained. In the fifth case, the closure is a positive response to a job well done – a job that has ensured that capacity remains within the neighbourhood. Groups do not have to last for ever and there may be good reasons for them to fade away or be replaced – as the snakes and ladders exercise showed, out of their ashes might come something new and more viable. But, some of these organisations left a gap that will not be easily filled and their demise represents a massive loss of resources in terms of funding, local knowledge and skills, commitment and energy.

A summer playscheme in Pickersleigh, Malvern. The neighbourhood organisation here was one of the smaller ones in the Programme

Why did the light touch work?

Measuring the benefits of a Programme like this is difficult. We used the action planning process to test whether Programme participants had progressed or not in relation to their aims. But scores were largely positive and based on self-assessment (albeit with facilitator and evaluator input) and the development stages in Table 5.1 (page 68) represent a composite assessment by the evaluation team. Measuring the impact in any other way would have been difficult for a number of reasons. First, there are attribution problems. Given the many other factors that affect the neighbourhoods concerned, it would be difficult to unravel the contribution that the Programme had made in terms of observable changes in the neighbourhood and clearly attribute these to such a small intervention. Second, the interventions were largely concerned with improving processes and confidence, both of which are difficult to pin down in any measurable form, especially when it is the group rather than an individual that is the unit of measurement.

Nonetheless, the evidence suggests that, in the majority of cases, the Programme had positive benefits. It also suggests that it was the following elements of the Programme that made a difference.

Programme design

- The Programme timescale and the continuous relationship between each project and its facilitator made it possible for facilitators to build relationships and trust, to reflect on how each project was developing, to pick up on emerging issues and therefore to suggest new directions. This continuous relationship also helped to provide continuity when key allies in the system moved on – a frequent occurrence in today's hyperactive policy environment.
- There did not have to be a 'problem' to trigger support and there was therefore more potential for a development role.
- Support from JRF came primarily through one person – this allowed for a more coordinated approach (rather than lots of people working with the same organisation). Facilitators made the other aspects of the Programme accessible, by supporting organisations in thinking through how to use credit, by making relevant information and knowledge accessible to the participating organisations, by running the action planning process and by encouraging organisations to attend networking events and supporting them when they were there.
- The package of resources meant that each element reinforced the others. For example, in their different ways, the availability of credit and the networking events helped to establish an affinity with the Programme. Participants also had access to other aspects of JRF's work, for example the National Regeneration Convention, which they might not have attended if they had not had personal contact with JRF.

Flexible approach

'Support that meets the needs of the group according to where they are in terms of development.' (Advisory group member)

- Facilitators were given the flexibility to use judgement and determine the balance between doing and enabling in each situation. Few funding programmes allow the flexibility for a group to change direction and to call on a different kind of help.
- Facilitators were also employed at arm's length – they were not JRF employees, which gave them greater independence from the Programme funding.

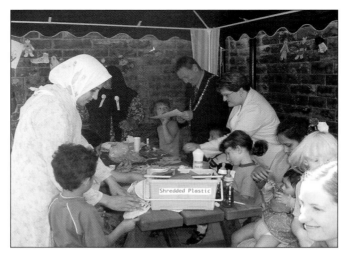

Todmorden in Calderdale: a summer playscheme organised by Integrate

- Credit could be used flexibly in response to the needs of the organisation; there were no strings attached and it was not tied to a financial year, which meant it could be used when appropriate to the organisation rather than being dependent on the funder's agenda and timescale.

Skills and experience

- There have been particular benefits from having facilitators 'of the region'. They are already linked into local and regional networks, have long-established useful contacts and understand some of the local context.
- The JRF was able to attract some highly skilled and experienced professionals to undertake the facilitation role, who had the experience, confidence and skills to be taken seriously by power holders ("someone with respect on your side").
- The benefits have been particularly high where organisations already knew and had worked with their facilitator or where a region-wide or country-wide policy has provided a focus for support.

A learning network

- The Programme was always clear that it valued the knowledge and experience of communities themselves. Through its networking events it was able to reduce the isolation many groups (and sometimes workers) felt. These events gave participants the power of knowing both that their problems were shared by organisations all over Britain and that their experience and support was valuable to others. This allowed learning across the Programme, between different organisations, but also between organisations and the facilitators, managers and evaluators associated with the Programme.
- The regularity of networking events enabled relationships and trust, and therefore confidence, to build over time. The events were well administered, planned and structured and had facilitation support from advisory group members, facilitators, the evaluators and the Programme manager.

  'We were able to view our fears without worrying because it was not in the local community, and we saw that others were suffering too, sometimes facing problems that we didn't.'

An (independent) friend in high places

- The JRF is independent from government and was therefore not driven by the need to deliver predetermined government policy goals. This allowed the Programme to address all aspects of empowerment and to be seen as an honest broker.
- The JRF is a recognised player at the national policy level – the facilitators brought the JRF name with them and the JRF name opened doors to mediation and brokerage that might not otherwise have been available.

Limitations

There were also things that did not work. The Programme's experience raises questions in particular about:

- *New technology* and how far we rely on it to empower community-based organisations – how many more websites do people actually need?
- *Networking opportunities* – while organisations like the opportunity to meet each other – at least once they have tried it – they rarely have the time and resources to take up all the opportunities on offer, especially if they are small and without paid staff.
- *Leadership* – it can be difficult to spread learning beyond one or two participants in a Programme, and tackling leadership issues proved to be a major challenge when people did not see the need to change or involve others.
- *Strategic vision* – although action planning helped, facilitators commented on the need to extend the vision of their organisations and enable them to see the wider picture – this might not be necessary for all neighbourhood organisations, but it is for those who wish to engage effectively with power holders.
- Getting power holders to *take community-based organisations seriously* – while the Programme was able to do a lot to break down barriers between its organisations and powerful stakeholders, there was still further to go. One facilitator, in a region where there were three small organisations in areas not covered by major regeneration

Concierge, Steve Cosgrove, on Edinburgh's Pilton estate

schemes, said: "In none of the three smaller projects is there yet a sustained and effective partnership between the local authority and any organisations established by the residents".

Tensions in the Programme

Running a programme that has some logic and a clear framework for engagement but also allows for flexibility and participant determination raises other questions about Programme design and how this kind of support could be replicated.

Light touch vis-à-vis challenge and sanctions

There were no sanctions in the JRF Programme and there are limits as to how much leverage a light touch programme can bring to bear. Tackling some of the more difficult issues such as leadership and the relationship with power holders, and even convincing smaller organisations to think more strategically, needed a more intensive engagement and a clearer – or more challenging – contract as to what was expected of Programme participants, as well as buy-in from partners.

Balancing flexibility with basic rules of engagement

In order to build a programme there need to be some rules of engagement. One of the 'rules' in this programme was the action planning requirement and, while even many of those who were unhappy about having to do this now talk about its value, this raised issues at the beginning about how to balance the need to challenge with the principle of group determination.

Building long-term relationships vis-à-vis pooling of skills and knowledge

We have highlighted the importance of committing time to the Programme development and the opportunity this provided for trust to be built between individual facilitators and the organisations they were matched with. Yet, the facilitators brought different skills and knowledge, and perhaps these could have been used more effectively if matched to the particular needs of organisations. A more flexible approach that permitted facilitators to bring in one of their peers where particular skills or knowledge were required would have allowed participants to combine the best of both approaches.

Finding the right match

What suited one organisation did not necessarily suit another – while some thrived on a flexible approach, others wanted more direction. Because of this, there was a minority of cases where the match between facilitator and organisation did not really work. While there were some advantages to regional working, it limited the scope to move facilitators around. In these rare cases, a change of facilitator would probably have allowed these organisations to gain more from the Programme. Any programme providing this kind of support over a fairly long period of time would need to provide for this eventuality.

Future policy implications

The JRF Neighbourhood Programme has now come to an end. It has not come up with any startling revelations or magic solutions to the challenges of community engagement. But its more subtle messages are nonetheless extremely significant for the success of future policy to engage communities and to tackle the implementation gap. These messages are that:

- the best and most exciting policy ideas will still falter if they are not backed up by the resources, levers and incentives to make them work;
- if neighbourhood working is to benefit *all* the most disadvantaged neighbourhoods, attention needs to be turned to pockets of disadvantage within more affluent areas that are often hidden from view and where authorities often do not have the experience, incentives or resources to engage in effective neighbourhood working;
- while there is no substitute for investment in long-term community development, especially in those areas with little history of such investment, a fairly low-level continuous input can make a difference.

In the remainder of this chapter, we draw on the experience of the 20 organisations in the Programme to look first at where support is most needed and what policy makers can do to maximise this support. We then consider where the support might come from, before ending with recommendations for national government, local public authorities and service providers and infrastructure bodies in government and the third sector.

A meeting of the Tenants and Residents Association in Castle Vale, Birmingham

The context

Current interest in devolving power can be expected to give people more opportunities to engage with official agencies in improving the services and decisions that affect their neighbourhoods. There is a commitment to the neighbourhood – although it takes different forms – in all three countries. There is also cross-party support. And while history shows us that the fortunes of neighbourhood as a policy focus fluctuate over time, it also shows us that it is a recurring theme.

As welcome as this commitment is, it demands a great deal of community-based organisations. There are lots of ideas around on techniques of engagement and triggers for holding politicians and services accountable. But the ultimate success of these initiatives – if they are not simply to strengthen the voice of the strongest – will depend on two things. The first is *sustained organisational capacity* in the most disadvantaged and damaged neighbourhoods – supporting informed residents in the communities to build sustainable, effective and accountable organisations. The second is *a culture within all public authorities that can engage and respond* to neighbourhood concerns in new ways.

Implications for policy I: Sustainable community-based organisations

The demands of neighbourhood working and of maintaining engagement across the different communities in a neighbourhood will require strong and sustainable organisations at neighbourhood level. But giving organisations time to work is also important – although many organisations go through rough patches, it does not mean they do not have a positive future. The experience from the Programme suggests five key ingredients for sustainable community-based organisations: a strong base of participation; the capacity to engage with diversity; effective leadership; a strategic plan with effective management systems; and sustainable funding.

A strong base of participation

A lot is expected of the people who are active in communities: to engage in new partnership processes; to develop social enterprises; to run their own services; to be good employers; and still to remain close to their roots in the local community. A surprising number of organisations manage to juggle all these expectations, but these demands can also expose organisational weaknesses.

Community organisations often rely on a handful of committed people and, while the increasing emphasis on community engagement is welcome, engaging with local agencies and decision makers relies even more on the few people who know the ropes and speak the language. Effective organisations therefore need to be able to draw on a pool of people from all parts of the community, who are active at neighbourhood level. Otherwise the range of community interests is unlikely to be represented and key activists will burn-out. The more is expected of them, the wider that pool of people needs to be. Yet, the work of the Programme has underlined the fragility of many local groups, especially in areas that have not benefited from major investment in neighbourhood renewal or capacity building. Many neighbourhood organisations rely on the efforts of very few individuals. It is easy to get used to operating as a small group, and we learnt that persuading volunteers who have run organisations almost single-handedly for many years to 'let go' requires time, trust and considerable skill. And while there are people in communities who block rather than facilitate engagement, it was also clear that many of the 'usual suspects' that partners condemn are created by unrealistic expectations on people's time and by the tendency of partners always to go back to the people they know.

St Pauls in bloom – two residents pictured in their amazing garden

Even where organisations want to get more people involved, many lack the confidence to do so – widening participation is a continual challenge for many organisations. Chapter 3 gives examples of the ways in which Programme participants tried to engage more people. At the same time, organisations need ideas, encouragement and resources to engage more widely; or they may need to be challenged to find ways of reaching more people. A trusted advisor can do this. Small amounts of money with no strings attached make it possible to lay on events and initiatives that reach a wider community. Opportunities for organisations to meet, share ideas and gain inspiration from each other can play a significant role in encouraging Programme participants 'not to give up'.

Engaging with diversity

The kinds of resources offered by the Programme also help neighbourhood organisations to cross divides, between different social groupings within neighbourhoods or between neighbourhoods themselves, finding common ground rather than competing for attention. The Programme suggests that many people in local groups find cohesion and diversity uncomfortable issues to acknowledge and address. But Chapter 3 shows how grassroots networking and 'whole' community events, the development of 'pioneer' services for excluded migrants, participatory consultation initiatives and strategic partnerships have helped to bridge these divides, as have explicit equalities policies and procedures for service delivery and representation. Events that can bring people together across potential ethnic, tenure and generational divides are particularly important, providing an informal foundation of 'bridging social capital' on which more formal coordinating arrangements can be built.

Our diversity 'joint project' suggested that starting from common ground rather than differences can be an effective basis for collaboration between diverse groups in the neighbourhood. Sometimes the common ground can be established by 'reframing' the way that local problems are defined, for example conflict between groups of youths of different ethnic origin can be defined as a community safety issue rather than as racial tension. It also suggests that building 'bridging capital' across social boundaries between people who have had quite separate lives cannot be expected to happen overnight. It takes "time and trust".

Fault-lines do not appear only between social groups but also between different initiatives competing for local attention and funds. While the Programme underlines the importance of mapping the territory before introducing new initiatives, it has also demonstrated the value of developing a protocol for joint working across a neighbourhood (see Resource sheet F).

Leadership

Effective leadership – the understanding and skills to build empowerment more widely – is crucial to successful neighbourhood development. But challenging leaders to share power – or supporting other group members to make these challenges or even set up on their own — requires considerable skill, trust and sensitivity. However, facilitation support combined with networking opportunities allowed leaders to discover the value of sharing responsibility: one person with a leading role in a neighbourhood organisation "learned I could share my responsibility for funding with other members of the group". Another agreed that "the pressure has come off me as we have shared the work".

The Programme has also illustrated the value of providing mentoring support for paid community workers, especially for those who are isolated or new to their posts. One worker who came into post during the Programme explained how as a new worker it gave him a 'kick start' and will continue to be valuable:

Chris Parsons (standing on the left): community leader, paid worker and chair of Scarborough's Eastfield Neighbourhood Partnership

'There has been a real personal benefit to me – a whole new network of friends and colleagues both at JRF and within the other neighbourhoods that I will be able to draw on for help, support, advice and information in the future.'

Strategic planning and management

Neighbourhood-based organisations operate within a complex environment where the pace of development is often determined by external funding imperatives. The accelerated pace of policy change nowadays takes little account of existing capacity and organisations can find themselves taking on new responsibilities and managing new enterprises and services without the management systems or facilities to match. Communities can be seduced by funding opportunities and do not always have the structures or the understanding to undertake the sophisticated risk analyses that new responsibilities bring with them. Some of the smaller organisations did not even have the systems to manage a small amount of credit and needed help to set up a bank account. It is easy to become distracted from the real purpose, especially when sums of money are involved. For organisations moving into social enterprise development, managing the finances can be a real headache. Several of the Programme participants were running social enterprises and even the most experienced community organisations were not immune to financial troubles, with two of our more established organisations folding because of financial difficulties. This represented a huge waste of energy, commitment and learning.

These issues are pertinent to all organisations that are in the process of growth, not just the larger ones. Many organisations move to employing staff but are often unprepared for the considerable responsibilities that go with employment and for the change in dynamics that employing people creates locally, whether new staff are local people or come from outside. At worst they can find themselves in deep water when things go wrong; more often both staff and volunteer managers feel insecure and undervalued. The potential range of options from accessing training around management and supervision skills, to bringing outside expertise onto the management committee or board of trustees, to

John Taylor, former local councillor and now a very active community leader in Swindon's Broad Street area

employment and secondment agreements with more sophisticated bodies, need to be made more widely available.

Despite initial misgivings on the part of many Programme participants, this report has demonstrated how action planning helped to provide a solid base for community organisations that otherwise struggled to keep up with changing agendas. Programme participants found that it helped them to refocus and prioritise what was in their best long-term interests. It reminded them where they might have strayed from their original intentions and gave them an opportunity to return to and review the relevance of their objectives in a planned rather than ad hoc way. Action planning also helped to support effective leadership by bringing the wider membership together to discuss plans and progress – thereby allowing more people to 'own' future development.

Sustainable resources

A good strategic plan also goes down well with funders. There are many guides to funding, and we do not intend to add to them here. But our funding 'joint project' suggested that the building of a sustainable organisation rests in part on the development of a good 'contact' network as well as the ability to think laterally. Resources do not always come in the form of cash.

BOX 5.1 A GOOD 'CONTACT NETWORK'

The **Boothtown Community Partnership** has a good 'contacts network' to call on. This includes links to Voluntary Action Calderdale for training and skills development, the council's museums and library service, and the council's street cleansing department over environmental matters. The development of the 'Boothtown Pod' community building also secured a number of donations in cash and kind from various private sector companies.

Government policy is encouraging communities to develop their own assets and enterprises, maybe taking on service contracts. But while some Programme participants were making this work, others were more cautious: organisations need a lot of skill and support to sustain this over the long term.

The compacts or equivalent agreements in each of the three countries make provision for sustainable funding policies and relationships and lay down basic principles which, if observed, would make a great deal of difference to the sustainability of neighbourhood organisations. However, as indicated in Chapter 1 there is considerable concern about the future funding context, particularly the likely consequences of the ending of SRB and European funding programmes. The interim report on the review of the third sector in England[16] is picking up this issue, and the concept that a minimum three-year funding becomes the norm is welcome, as is the understanding expressed in the local government White Paper[17] that grant aid funding for smaller organisations is essential. But suggestions as to where this money might come from appear to be elusive.

The following general *recommendations for sustainable community-based organisations* emerge from this and other material in the report:

---

[16] HM Treasury and Cabinet Office (2006)
[17] DCLG (2006a)

Lyn Sharry, Neighbourhood Renewal worker with St Pauls Unlimited Community Partnership, out with residents near the Family and Learning Centre

- Widespread engagement needs to be resourced, otherwise, participation will continue to depend on the few.
- Support is also needed for paid community workers, especially when they are working in isolation.
- Investment in the voluntary and community sector infrastructure is essential if neighbourhood-based organisations are to be effective and accountable.
- It is important to have access to mediation in a policy environment where competition for funding and attention can drive wedges between communities.
- Calls for community engagement and participation should always be accompanied by resources ('a percentage for participation').
- All authorities should develop a community development strategy in consultation with local groups that would encompass the requirements above. This would be an informed strategy that goes beyond and underpins the call for community engagement strategies in England and similar calls for community engagement in Scotland and Wales.

What else policy makers can do

- It is important to have realistic expectations, especially in neighbourhoods where people are struggling to survive or to reconcile the needs of diverse and fragmented communities.
- Encouraging community organisations to plan is important but funders should be flexible in their requirements for strategic and business plans. Otherwise, organisations will be trying to work to a range of different plans to suit the needs of a whole range of funders.
- New initiatives should take account of the assets and resources that already exist on the ground and build on these as far as possible.
- New opportunities for participation should also take account of other local initiatives and ensure that demands for community participation are streamlined.

Implications for policy II: A responsive and engaged public sector culture

One Programme participant wrote that:

'Even where they have built up a strong local organisation, neighbourhoods face real challenges in securing the right of their neighbourhood to be positively engaged in decisions taken by the power structures which affect quality of life in the neighbourhood.'

Another went on to highlight:

'... the continuing failure of public authorities to understand how communities operate (with all their complexity and confusion) and for them [local authorities] to adapt their ways of working to be more responsive, more generous and more trusting towards community members.'

There are inevitable tensions between existing power structures and community organisations who want to maintain the right to challenge as well as find ways of working with decision makers and service providers for the benefit of the community. The evidence from the Programme suggests that community organisations as well as power holders need to be challenged if a new settlement is to be reached at neighbourhood level. Several of the Programme participants have increased their knowledge about how the system works and have more confidence in dealing with power holders. Some are winning over previously sceptical local authorities just by 'being good at what they do'. However, the Programme has also shown that, although progress can be made on a case-by-case basis, power holders readily revert to

A visit to Caia Park in Wrexham, where the local partnership delivers a wide range of services: 70% of its employees are residents

traditional ways of doing things, that relationships are still dependent on individuals and that there are issues that still need to be resolved. In one region alone:

- One organisation that is planning to expand its building is trying to come to terms with council resistance and inertia over its plans.
- Another whose funding is coming to an end is having to deal with unhelpful council departments and local competition for resources.
- A third has been hit by major plans for its estate on which there has been no consultation and which have been kept so secret that the organisation has not even been able to reveal that it knows about them to residents.

On the other hand, it is important to recognise that the 'power holders' are not a homogeneous group. Even where relationships have been patchy, there have usually been allies to work with or to intercede for the neighbourhood. The local authority events also provided examples where successful community engagement had benefited both the community and the council itself.

BOX 5.2 WORKING EFFECTIVELY TOGETHER

In Wales, for example:

- a community organisation was able (thanks to earlier community development work) to carry out a consultation exercise for the council at only two days' notice. This allowed the council to respond successfully to a major funding opportunity and secure funding for important new community facilities;
- the transfer of the freehold of a previously disused leisure centre to community control will enable residents in a severely disadvantaged area to attract investment for a desperately needed new health centre and pharmacy;
- an attempted press campaign against a council-backed project to renovate an old chapel backfired when residents protested that this was what the community wanted – and that they had carried out a consultation exercise to prove it.

The experience of the Programme (including the events that it held with local authorities and others) suggests that the key elements of a change in culture are: informal opportunities for learning between public authorities and local residents; resources for brokerage; structures that enable neighbourhood working; the time for things to work; and support and incentives for staff and members working directly with communities.

Informal opportunities for learning between public authorities and local residents

There were examples of capacity-building approaches within the Programme that benefited both communities and public bodies, for instance a successful approach to mutual learning between community activists and housing officers in Pilton, 'job swaps' in Boscombe, which in one case found a council chief executive taking a temporary post as a frontline care worker, and the secondment opportunity for a local authority manager in Plymouth provided by the Tamar Development Trust. In addition to seeing what it is like "from another's shoes", job swaps and secondments also enable personal relationships and hence trust (social capital) to develop between partners.

Resources for brokerage

Brokerage was not something that was designed into the Programme but a need that emerged from it. Chapter 4 has described in detail why it was needed and what it delivered. An independent outsider whom all parties respect is a valuable resource in helping to turn a stalemate into a win–win situation. Chapter 4 suggests that effective brokerage is reliant on:

- the 'broker' being familiar with the issues and understanding the historical, policy and local context;
- preparation beforehand to ensure that all stakeholders have had an opportunity to feed their perspective into the agenda;
- clarity at the end of the meeting on what will happen next;
- opportunities for the community to get together afterwards and 'debrief';
- keeping the group centre stage and not 'taking over'.

Structures for neighbourhood working

The recent English local government White Paper[18] and the Scottish Community Planning system both provide for sub-local partnerships – in the English case at neighbourhood level. Although many local authorities have area structures, however, few have the systems in place at present to devolve to neighbourhood level, especially outside the big unitary authorities.

BOX 5.3 DEVOLVING TO NATURAL NEIGHBOURHOODS

A keynote presentation by the chief executive of Aberdeen City Council to one of the local authority events highlighted how concerted leadership to empower citizens and neighbourhoods is paying benefits in that city. The programme includes:

- decentralisation of the council sees most officers working in new area offices, headed by area corporate directors;
- reorganisation of the old departments along thematic lines;
- empowerment of 37 'natural' (ie logical to residents) neighbourhoods for action planning;
- reorganisation of ward and statutory community council boundaries to conform to those of neighbourhoods, bringing the council's community development expertise within the chief executive's unit; and
- a 'citizens parliament' ('The Civic Forum') of 120 representatives of neighbourhoods and communities of interest, which works for community benefit on key partnerships and strategy groups.

The natural neighbourhoods emerged out of a process of dialogue between community organisations and service providers lasting about one year. Having gone through that process, residents are pleased that their concerns and perceptions have been recognised, while service providers (particularly the police) are moving towards use of coterminous neighbourhood (and area) boundaries for service provision.

One note of caution, however, is that significant change of this kind is not an easy or a quick process. It requires space for negotiation with all those affected – communities and service providers – and it ultimately rests on 'buy-in' and determined leadership.

---

[18] DCLG (2006a)

Gellideg in Merthyr Tydfil, a natural community where devolving powers to a neighbourhood organisation is paying great dividends

The Programme also highlighted the problems of partnership proliferation. The costs in people energy are high: "participants are heavily burdened from participating in a merry-go-round of partnerships"; they speak of "initiative fatigue", "fragmentation", "confusion" and "too many talking shops". Pilton achieved a community-driven model of partnership with a strategic agenda involving community members and key stakeholders. This contrasted with the situation in another area in which a partnership funded by the RDA was attempting to work alongside a second, centrally funded, neighbourhood management partnership with different boundaries and a third community health partnership supported by another funding stream.

Another learning point in relation to structure came from the same organisation. Its initial board was far too large to be workable. When a local partnership is established, the first inclination is to invite every relevant organisation to meetings. But a balance is needed between inclusiveness and efficiency. Experience from this organisation suggests that a board with more than 20 members is seldom functional.

The time for things to work

Time is a recurring theme throughout this and most other accounts of neighbourhood working. Programme participants noted that partnerships may take one or two years to resolve initial tensions and to build the relationships and trust necessary to work jointly on common agendas between community interests and institutional stakeholders. In one neighbourhood, an SRB-funded partnership that had been particularly slow to get started was winding up just as it was, at last, getting into its stride.

Rhianon Passmore of Ty Sign – a local councillor, resident in the community, whose efforts were instrumental in helping the local partnership to grow

Support and incentives for staff and members working at neighbourhood level

Programme participants suggested that it also yielded benefits for a number of the other stakeholders working with their organisations.

New policies, especially in England, place great emphasis on the role of ward councillors in neighbourhood working. This came up as a critical issue in all three of the Programme's local authority events and will inform another JRF initiative focused on working with frontline councillors.

BOX 5.4 THE CHANGING ROLE OF COUNCILLORS: COMMON ISSUES FROM THE THREE LOCAL AUTHORITY EVENTS

Councillors can feel threatened and uncertain as a result of continuing changes in local government, especially when community representatives have growing expectations of their own significance in neighbourhood governance. Tensions are not uncommon between councillors who see theirs as the key role in representing local interests and residents who are acting as community leaders or representatives. Local residents may feel that some local councillors are committed to party interests (or even their own) at the expense of neighbourhood interests.

Representative and participatory democracy are both vital to the democratic process, and councillors have an important job to do in supporting and promoting the neighbourhood agenda. Working with local councillors to help them define a more sophisticated community leadership role, complementary to community activism, is essential to the success of current local government policies.

At the Welsh event it was suggested that councillors could have an enabling role linking community organisations to appropriate officers and vice versa. However, there was also concern that councillors were often not aware of the priorities across different departments of the local authority and would need training to play this role effectively.

The Scottish event suggested that councillors would have a natural overview across neighbourhoods, which would help to find areas of common cause. It also saw an important role for local councillors in championing neighbourhood action plans within the broader governance structure.

Further general *recommendations for a responsive and engaged public sector* are:

- A cross-departmental strategic approach to neighbourhood development is needed at national government level, which connects explicitly with arrangements in England for signing off LAAs, in Scotland with CPPs and Regeneration Outcome Agreements, and in Wales with Public Service Agreements and Spatial Plans.
- Some authorities have cabinet members with portfolios covering communities and the third sector; an equivalent to the Minister for the Third Sector at local authority level (and in other public bodies) could do much to ensure a strategic and coordinated approach.
- Neighbourhoods need to have a real identity for both those who live *and* those who work there.
- Care needs to be taken not to overburden neighbourhoods with forums, committees and partnerships.
- Capacity building is needed across all sectors to drive the culture change required to implement the neighbourhoods agenda – this should include joint training with community organisations, job swaps and secondments.
- Effective engagement with communities also needs to be incentivised and rewarded through performance management systems, local authority agreements and promotion systems.

Several of the earlier learning points relating to the development of sustainable community organisations also have implications for public authorities.

Enjoying the sun: taking the kids out for a stroll on the edge of Scarborough's very large out-of-town Eastfield estate

Replicating the light touch model

Neighbourhood-based organisations have a major contribution to make to neighbourhood change, both strategically and operationally. But they cannot do it alone, and the challenges of too few resources and the often poor relationships with institutional partners have been well documented in this report. We therefore need to focus on approaches to delivering support to all partners involved in the regeneration of neighbourhoods, bearing in mind that there is no one recipe for effective working in neighbourhoods.

BOX 5.5 BUILDING LOCAL PARTNER CAPACITY

In Wales, the national administration has maintained a direct role in promoting community engagement and capacity building through its continued funding for Communities First; in England and Scotland, this is largely devolved through LAAs and CPPs. In England, in particular, the ward councillor will be crucial to the ability of local community organisations to turn the intentions of the White Paper into practice, given their central role in triggering new accountability mechanisms and in administering new local budgets. While in principle this has the potential to strengthen local democracy significantly, finding ways of ensuring this happens across the whole country will be a major challenge for local government infrastructure organisations. Government offices, meanwhile, need also to have the skills to ensure that LAAs are an effective route through which to ensure community engagement both happens and is adequately resourced.

In one of the networking events, we asked the Programme participants where they looked to for help; the action planning process also explored where participants might get help in the future. This suggested that answers may come from a variety of sources, some very local and some national. But when asked what resources they would still need but didn't know where to go for them, it became clear that for many organisations, it was going to be difficult to find the following, much-appreciated, resources:

Street scene in East Pollokshields, Glasgow

- *Facilitation*
  - Mentoring and long-term development support

- *Credit*
  - Small 'getting started' grants

- *Information*
  - Information about local authority policy pertinent to neighbourhoods
  - Access to a pool of policies and procedures that organisations can adopt
  - A coordinated route map for local and regional training opportunities and mechanisms to help organisations identify their training needs

- *Being taken seriously by power holders*
  - Joint training for local authorities and communities
  - Neighbourhood enquiries – mini/local scrutiny to address problems/barriers
  - Partnership mediation and independent brokers with resources, influence and experience who can help break down barriers
  - Complaints desk

Light touch support should not be seen as an alternative to more substantial community development support, especially in areas with little history of neighbourhood organisation and investment. However, it does have an important contribution to make as part of a package of support to neighbourhood working. But how can it be provided?

Roughly speaking, the cost of the support provided by the Neighbourhood Programme came to £7,500 per neighbourhood per year. If this were provided by a single funder, it would translate into:

- £150,000 per annum for a town with 20 deprived neighbourhoods; or
- £2.25 million per annum for a region with 300 deprived neighbourhoods.

One of Norfolk Park's strongest assets: its fine view across the city of Sheffield

There are various potential sources of light touch support that could be pooled at local and/or regional level (see Table 5.2, page 92). They would, however, need to be part of a coherent strategy, coordinated at regional and Local Strategic Partnership (LSP) level and recognising the kind of support best provided at each level. Coordination and a strategic approach are vital in providing light touch support that is accessible and appropriate to neighbourhood organisations; that is, such support should not be dependent on the willingness or capacity of individual local authorities nor result in a scramble for resources on the part of the neighbourhood organisations.

While some elements could be provided at any level (information is the obvious example), others lend themselves to particular spatial scales. For example, the experience of the Single Community Programme suggests that credit is best administered at city- or district-wide level, especially if it is to be embedded in support and networking opportunities in the way that Programme funds were.[19] The experience of the Neighbourhood Programme suggests that networking opportunities need to take place at regional and national level to maximise learning. While there are opportunities for neighbourhood-based groups to attend existing conferences, the Neighbourhood Programme experience suggests that effective networking takes time to build – these events only begin to feel safe and comfortable to participants after they have been a few times and got the measure of them. Regional voluntary and community sector (VCS) networks could replicate this, as national membership organisations already do, to a certain degree (especially those that pay attention to the social side of the conference). Events like this also provide opportunities for neighbourhood organisations to interact informally with policy makers and to break down barriers. Investment in attendance at these conferences therefore has a value that few funders appreciate.

Alison Hill from Caia Park Partnership in Wrexham and Neil Poulton from Boscombe Working Community Partnership in Bournemouth, who both valued the 'light touch' support their organisations received during the JRF Programme

[19] ODPM (2005)

The experience of the Programme suggests that brokerage roles are more likely to be effective if based at a regional level. This allows the broker to be outside local politics but to have some local knowledge and contacts. In England, the government's own Neighbourhood Renewal advisors have been attached to government offices of the regions. Regional VCS networks and Regional Centres of Excellence might also provide a suitable base. What this would involve would be a register of approved brokers and funding to support their use (along the lines of the Neighbourhood Renewal advisor service).

Overall, however, we would suggest that it is the location of facilitation/mentoring support that is critical, given that this often acts as the route to all other forms of support. The availability of independent monitoring support for community activists and for paid workers can make an important contribution to the development of leadership skills and ultimately to organisational strength. The 'critical friend' role is rarely available to frontline development or community workers and even harder to access for activists. Access to a pool of people who can provide this would be invaluable to many working at neighbourhood level.

Turning this around, Table 5.2 suggests that the following organisations might have a role to play in providing future light touch support.

Local authorities

Local authorities are expected to play a strong community leadership role in all three countries. As the elected authorities, this is appropriate. However, many still need to learn to facilitate and enable. They also need to be freed from some of the centrally imposed targets that tie their hands, while at the same time being provided with incentives to promote community engagement.

Statutory strategic partnerships

A key player in each country will be the multi-agency strategic partnership at local level (the LSP in England, the CPP in Scotland, and the Community Strategic Partnership or proposed Public Service Board in Wales). Some level of community involvement is required in each, as well as in the plans they produce. If this is to be a genuine opportunity to engage communities in determining the future of their services from the bottom up (rather than a tick-box exercise), a community development strategy as outlined above and in Chapter 6 will be essential. In England, the LAA stronger communities indicators on voice and influence provide a useful mechanism for measuring performance.

Regional bodies

In England there are a number of regional bodies that currently play a role in providing access to learning opportunities and can help to bring partners together. These include government offices, the RDA, the Regional Centres of Excellence and regional structures for local government. Many run training courses, action learning sets and provide knowledge-based information. In Scotland and Wales these roles are likely to be played by national bodies.

Table 5.2 Potential sources of light touch support

Type of support	Who could deliver?	At what level?
Facilitation/mentoring	Voluntary and community sector infrastructure	City- or district-wide
Action planning support	Government offices through Neighbourhood Renewal advisors	Regional (or national in the devolved administrations)
Peer mentoring	Community anchor organisations; RSLs	Neighbourhood level
Credit (with support in applying for/spending it)	Community Foundations where they exist Statutory strategic partnerships at local level in the three countries	City- or district-wide (close enough for local knowledge, but removed from immediate neighbourhood politics)
Networking	Voluntary and community sector infrastructure	National Regional
Access to information	Already well catered for (although facilitator can help with sifting); Regional Centres of Excellence; the Academy for Sustainable Communities (England); the Centre for Regeneration (Scotland) the Communities First Support Network (Wales)	
Mediation and brokerage	Neighbourhood Renewal advisors	Regional (best to be independent of the day-to-day involvement)
Strategic coordination	Together We Can; Neighbourhood Management network; Communities First Support Network ; Academy for Sustainable Communities/ Scottish Centre for Regeneration; Regional Centres of Excellence	National Regional
	LSP partners – as part of LAA delivery; CPPs; Community Strategic Partnerships in Wales	Local

Government offices in England

It is important to ensure that people within those government agencies that sign off new LAAs, Community Plans and Public Service Plans have the knowledge and skills to draw on to ensure that these agreements deliver on community engagement. The network of independent Neighbourhood Renewal advisors in England is a valuable resource in this respect and also provides another model of mediation, brokerage and 'the critical friend'. It could have a significant role to play in providing generalist light touch and brokerage support in relation to the new agreements, especially where there are concerns about local relationships. In the context of a regional engagement strategy, this resource could also be expanded, complementing the role of other local players and linked to an imaginative use of neighbourhood credit to back ideas and build energy and capacity.

Housing associations

Within the Programme, housing associations are likely to be an important source of follow-on support for Programme participants. In Malvern, a good relationship with the main social landlord – the Elgar Housing Association – has helped to boost local confidence and provide some resources, while in East Pollokshields, Southside Housing Association has kick-started a whole range of developments such as the community newsletter and information gathering across the diverse neighbourhood. Local social landlords have also been significant players in Lodge Farm and Eastfield. Castle Vale Housing Action Trust, of course, is already a community-based housing association.[20]

BOX 5.6 THE CONTRIBUTION OF HOUSING ASSOCIATIONS

In **Malvern**, where community engagement is very fragile and resources for community development are few and far between, the support of the local housing association has been critical in increasing local confidence and supporting the local authority's own community worker, who is quite isolated within her own organisation. Good relations with the police have also secured funding through community safety legislation to support further work with the local community.

In **Southside**, it was the local housing association that initiated the community needs survey that led the development of the East Pollokshields Partnership and potentially much greater resident influence over the community planning process in Glasgow.

Near the offices of Southside Housing Association in East Pollokshields

[20] Housing associations as 'community anchors' are discussed in Housing Associations Charitable Trust (2006).

National infrastructure bodies

National bodies in the third sector and in the statutory sector have a valuable role to play. Third sector infrastructure organisations already run conferences and briefing/consultation events that local organisations can tap into, as well as providing knowledge resources. In the public sector, the LGAs in each country and the IDA (in England) have also provided guidance and training opportunities for their members in community engagement and working with different partners. They might also consider whether there is an equivalent to the light touch support available to communities through this Programme that could be provided for public sector personnel working with residents in disadvantaged neighbourhoods.

The third sector infrastructure

Government in England has committed itself to the support of the third sector infrastructure through Change Up and Capacity Builders. It is essential that these initiatives in England and parallel initiatives in Scotland and Wales invest in the capacity of the infrastructure to support voice as well as service delivery. In England, regional and sub-regional Change Up strategies should provide an ideal opportunity for building in this kind of support. In all three countries, local and regional bodies are well placed to act as 'resource centres', dispensing credit and developing a network of facilitators who could be 'at the end of a phone' and who would be available for mediation in a crisis. However, experience suggests that facilitation should be independent of any single organisation or sector, and that facilitators should bring regional or national experience with them. There is a value, too, in brokers not being from the immediate locality. This may mean that facilitation and mediation is best provided at regional level.

Lord Rooker with community wardens in Castle Vale

Community anchor organisations

These are area- or neighbourhood-based organisations that provide some infrastructure resource and support to smaller groups as well as usually providing a focus for community development/neighbourhood change. In England, Castle Vale Housing Action Trust is one of the government-supported Guide Neighbourhoods set up to test and develop this idea, and the larger organisations from the Programme in Scotland and Wales certainly have the capacity to play a similar role.

Community foundations

Since the demise of the Community Chest and Community Learning Chest in most parts of England, community foundations are the most promising long-term hope for small grants with no strings attached (but with the support that credit in this Programme and the Community Chest provided). But community foundations do not exist everywhere – their coverage is patchy, so alternatives need to be found. Serious consideration needs to be given to ways of ensuring that this kind of financial support is available through the LAA and through other programmes. All the evidence suggests that it is a major way of spreading involvement at neighbourhood level.[21]

---

[21] ODPM (2005)

6

Learning for the future: summary and recommendations

Lisa Blackwood and Musnilya Babatunji of St Pauls Unlimited at a JRF networking event

Over the past 10 years, finding new ways of engaging citizens with democracy and making services more responsive to the people who use them have been common themes with policy makers across Britain. The way this has been expressed in policy differs across the three national administrations in Britain but there is a common interest in neighbourhood working in order to give communities the opportunity to do things for themselves as well making service providers and policy makers more accountable. Policy has also emphasised the need to change mainstream services rather than relying solely on special initiatives.

The three national administrations in England, Scotland and Wales have developed a range of programmes and structures to make this possible. However, while the language of policy has changed considerably and there is a growing repertoire of tools and triggers to strengthen the citizen voice, the work of this Programme suggests that not enough is changing for residents at ground level, especially in the most disadvantaged neighbourhoods. There is still an 'implementation gap'. The Programme has also drawn our attention to the problems faced by neighbourhoods that are outside acknowledged centres of deprivation and by authorities with limited experience in tackling exclusion at neighbourhood level.

Following the progress of 20 very different neighbourhood organisations and organisations across the three countries for a period of four years in all – together with a team of experienced facilitators – has given us a unique opportunity to explore the opportunities and challenges of Neighbourhood Renewal from a community perspective. As well as testing out 'light touch' ways of offering support to community organisations, this range of experience has also allowed us to find out how different policies are working out on the ground, what it is realistic to expect of local residents and what needs to happen at agency level in order to address the 'implementation gap'. In this final chapter, we summarise the main findings from this experience and pull out the implications for different players in the Neighbourhood Renewal field.

In Chapter 5, we suggested that engaging communities fully in the services and decisions that affect their lives would require two things:

- sustained organisational capacity, especially in the most disadvantaged neighbourhoods; and
- a responsive and engaged public sector culture.

What can partners and supporters do to ensure that these basic foundations for engagement are in place?

Sustainable organisational capacity

The experience of the Programme suggests that sustained organisational capacity requires:
- a strong base of participation;
- the capacity to engage with the diversity of local communities;
- effective leadership and accountability;
- a strategic action plan with effective management systems; and
- sustainable resources.

Public open space improved by Boscombe Working Community Partnership

Participation

The Programme came up with two contradictory findings on participation. The first emphasised the achievements of local residents and their considerable resourcefulness when it comes to getting their neighbourhoods involved in improving the quality of local life and services. But what also struck us was the fragility of many local organisations, especially in neighbourhoods that have been bypassed by the main Neighbourhood Renewal and Regeneration programmes.

Diverse communities

Building bridges across the generations, between different ethnic and faith groups and across other potential faultlines is essential in today's society. Where organisations have recognised the need to do this they have been considerably strengthened and their legitimacy with partners has deepened. But there are many factors in the external environment that can undermine this and partners need to be aware of these. Competitive funding often encourages competition or pits organisations against each other, while the media can worsen already charged situations.

Leadership

Leaders within the neighbourhood are expected to be dynamic and make things happen and at the same time to manage increasingly complex organisations, to be good employers, to engage the diversity of local people, and to link effectively with external agencies. The Programme worked with some excellent leaders, who were filling a role that few others wished to take on and who were doing their best to be accountable. Partners need to have realistic expectations, to be aware of the pressures on these people's lives and, above all, to recognise that they can only be expected to engage fully with their communities if communities are resourced to do so.

Effective management

The increasing emphasis on community management of services and assets will create new demands on communities' capacity to manage effectively. Managing the demands of growth will be a particular challenge for smaller groups, many of whom struggle with effective financial management. But this is an issue for larger organisations too. Organisations in the Programme discovered to their cost that this is an area of operation where trust is never enough.

What can help with this? Community accounting support has a long history and needs to be encouraged but the experience of the Programme also underlines the importance of effective auditing. Demands for monitoring from funders are often excessive and disproportionate, but this is one area where proper checks and balances are needed to ensure that organisations do not go into crisis.

Organisations also need support to consider their options around processes for recruitment, management and supervision of staff. The bonus of a paid worker can translate into a burden if effective systems are not in place.

Sustainable resources

Resources are about more than cash, for example organisations need support to network and build contacts, although they also need committed funds. Strategic development rests on longer-term funding agreements. Some organisations are moving into income-generating activities but this requires a additional range of business management skills and knowledge. There will always be a need for grant aid funding, particularly for smaller organisations.

A responsive and engaged public sector

The experience of the Programme suggests that a responsive and engaged public sector would be characterised by:

- structures for neighbourhood working that are real to the people who live there;
- support and incentives for officers and councillors;
- informal opportunities for learning and dialogue;
- allowing the time and continuity for changes to work and trust to be built.

The success of community engagement ultimately depends on the commitment of both officers and members at local level. However, it is widely recognised that this commitment is still patchy across authorities, across services and at individual level. While there are a growing number of authorities and public sector personnel who do acknowledge the importance – and added value – of working with communities, there are still many public bodies that are unsure how to go about it, while some remain very resistant. The Programme has demonstrated that this is particularly likely in authorities that have not to date been involved in Neighbourhood Renewal and Regeneration programmes.

Building trust takes time: a mix of residents and council officers at a meeting of Scarborough's Eastfield Neighbourhood Partnership

The capacity of local authorities to engage people is also affected by the pace of policy change. Trust depends on forging relationships with key individuals and individuals in the public sector often move very quickly. If continuity is not feasible, then the links have to be spread more widely and engagement needs to be built into the culture through induction, training (particularly joint training), secondments, promotion requirements, executive appointments and supervision. While the tools exist to do this with officers, if the local authority is willing to use them, getting those councillors to take up training and other opportunities can be more of a challenge. Some still find it difficult to reconcile their role as an elected councillor with the need to engage communities. The three countries face different challenges in this respect, but in all three, local government infrastructure bodies – preferably working in partnership with the relevant infrastructure organisations from the community sector – will have a critical role to play in both promoting good practice and challenging failure effectively. They might also consider how the kind of light touch support the Programme has provided for communities could be provided for officers and councillors with a particular brief to work with communities.

How light touch support can help

What the JRF Neighbourhood Programme was able to demonstrate was how a little mentoring, a small pot of money and the opportunity to meet with other neighbourhood organisations across the three countries could make a significant difference in addressing these challenges. The light touch resources it provided and the flexibility with which they were applied demonstrated the value of:

- action planning;
- a critical friend and a trusted voice at the end of a phone (or email);
- the injection of new ideas or knowledge about what had been tried elsewhere;
- support and mentoring for isolated community workers, so that they could better support local residents;

"No, we're supposed to be in that workshop over there!" Facilitator Jenny Lynn with Norfolk Park's Joan Hubbard at a networking event

- resources with no strings attached that could be spent when the group needed them;
- an ally when needed to support groups in negotiations with funders or other local organisations;
- opportunities to meet other people like them and share experience (peer support);
- the confidence of being 'kitemarked' by a respected organisation.

The kind of light touch support provided by the Programme is not enough on its own. It did not work everywhere. Some organisations resisted change; one or two did not really need what JRF had to offer. A few needed more help than the Programme could offer. But this Programme has demonstrated the value of light touch support as one indispensable component of a more comprehensive package alongside community development resources and more specialist technical support. As an advisory group member said:

'Small groups can do amazing things but they do need some (intensive) support in their early stages to help them focus, plan, organise, learn and deal with conflicts. In later stages, this support can become more light touch as long as it is still around and can be accessed where necessary.'

Recommendations

We began this report with the statement 'Neighbourhoods are important' and pointed to strategies implemented across England, Scotland and Wales that have focused on poverty and fragmentation at this level. The JRF Neighbourhood Programme has shown how its hallmark flexible light touch approach can complement and add value to current policies and strategies, giving people in deprived neighbourhoods the opportunity to engage more effectively with policies and services.

Presentation day in Boscombe: Neil Poulton from the Boscombe Working Community Partnership with volunteers at a Family Support Group

Light touch support is most likely to be effective if it is part of a broader community development strategy, which encompasses community empowerment, civic engagement and organisational development (as highlighted by the Department for Communities and Local Government in *The community development challenge*).[22] We recommend that such strategies should be adopted at both local and regional level to cover the following:

- a mapping of what is out there – both the strategies, organisations and activities that are already contributing and the resources that are available to the range of local communities;
- priorities and gaps;
- provision for intensive support to those neighbourhoods that need it;
- a percentage for participation:
  - to enable community organisations to engage;
  - to invest in the infrastructure;
- provision for light touch support to community-based organisations;
- approaches that provide for peer support among active community members;
- adequate support for local community workers, neighbourhood managers and other neighbourhood-based workers;
- support and incentives for public sector players (including guidelines as to how engagement would be monitored);
- where to go when things go wrong (mediation and brokerage).

It is important that regional and local strategies are linked for two reasons. First, some resources may be best provided at regional level – this applies particularly to facilitation, mediation and brokerage, while peer support through regional networks would also be

---

[22] DCLG (2006b)

valuable. Second, tackling the problems of disadvantaged neighbourhoods in particular needs to be embedded in regional approaches to planning, public health and economic development, and this will only happen if regional bodies see the significance of neighbourhoods and community engagement in developing their own policies.

In Chapter 5, we suggested some of the people/organisations who could provide either the whole light touch package or part of it:

- RSLs;
- a revamped Neighbourhood Renewal advisor service attached to government offices or regional networks (with appropriately skilled advisors);
- community anchor organisations – experienced community-based organisations with skills and knowledge to share (with appropriate resources);
- the voluntary and community sector infrastructure (with support from Capacity Builders in England, Communities First in Wales and Communities Scotland);
- community foundations.

Regional bodies (for example, Regional Centres of Excellence, government offices and regional networks) and local agencies and partnerships could take on the strategic coordination role. In Scotland and Wales, it might be appropriate to do this at national level. However, there is also an important role for national organisations in the third sector and the local government sector to play in benchmarking good practice, encouraging peer support and providing incentives and peer pressure to encourage the stragglers into line. It is particularly important to remember that this is not just a resource for the 88 most disadvantaged neighbourhoods – it is needed anywhere where there is a gap to be closed between the more affluent areas and those that do not share that affluence.

So what does this add up to?

Recommendations for community organisations

- Neighbourhood organisations must have financial checks and balances in place. Independent audit, preferably by auditors with experience in the sector, is essential, and the audit should be put out to tender on a regular basis. Organisations should seek help from their local council for voluntary service or similar body.
- Local organisations need to be aware of the responsibilities they are taking on when they employ staff and where to go if they get into difficulties. It helps to bring someone onto the recruitment panel who has experience in recruiting and employing staff. The Programme has also shown the importance of ensuring that managers have mentoring support external to the organisation. When local people are employed, there may be particular challenges as staff and volunteers sort out their new roles and responsibilities. It is vital to seek help early if things are not working out.
- Community representatives need to ensure that they communicate effectively with their constituency and are as accountable as they can be with the resources they have. Community organisations need also to consider how to build the succession and spread leadership tasks. This helps to strengthen the legitimacy of the organisation with outsiders as well as preventing burn-out. Shadowing and opportunities to meet less formally with external partners can be one way of interesting a wider pool of people.

Recommendations for voluntary and community sector infrastructure bodies

- As the liabilities and complexities of management increase, help with accounting, especially for smaller groups, needs to be seen as a vital resource.

Shopping therapy – Southside Housing Association's community worker Smina Akhtar takes a well-earned break in Pollokshields

- Community groups also need access to good advice on employment, especially during recruitment and the probationary period, and 'somewhere to go' if things start to go wrong.
- Mentoring support is invaluable to help community organisations – for both paid and unpaid workers – to meet the considerable demands they face, while spreading responsibility and ensuring accountability. Local infrastructure bodies are in a particularly good position to ensure that local organisations are informed about regional resources.
- Infrastructure bodies need to ensure that they are reaching all parts of the sector.

Recommendations for local partners

- Local partners need to have realistic expectations of community representatives and ensure that they are resourced to do their job. This will be a particularly important requirement in England where, as more and more power is devolved downwards to local authorities, it is local authorities who need to provide these resources.
- Local authorities should take a lead in ensuring that the LSP has a community development strategy with resources to match and commitment from all partners.
- As there is more and more encouragement to transfer services to the third sector, funders need to be aware of the challenges that face organisations as they grow and take on staff. The compact in each country provides guidance on the terms and conditions of funding that will support local organisations, and government funders are moving to three-year funding as the norm. There are plans to provide procurement training for commissioners in England. But local partners need to be aware of the challenges they face and be prepared to support them in taking on these new responsibilities, if their investment is to be maximised.

- Partners need to audit policies – especially funding policies – to ensure that they do not inadvertently drive wedges between communities.

Recommendations for regional bodies and national government

- There is a limit to what can be achieved at neighbourhood level. Regional bodies should monitor the impact of their policies on the most disadvantaged neighbourhoods in their region and ensure that action is being taken to close the gap.
- Regional bodies should work with local capacity-building networks to build a community development strategy that can provide community organisations in the region (and those in public sector bodies that have a community engagement role) with access to light touch facilitation, mediation and peer support.
- Governments should consider how the role of Neighbourhood Renewal advisors – on the English model – could be used to support the development of LAAs, Community Plans and Public Service Agreements that take full account of the voices from neighbourhoods.

Recommendations for national infrastructure bodies

The local government infrastructure in each country has a critical role in ensuring that adequate support is offered to neighbourhoods and that community voices are heard. Good work is already being done to publicise good practice in relation to community engagement. This needs to continue and, in England, the Local Government Association and the Improvement and Development Agency need to work with regional networks to ensure that the local authorities that most need support are being targeted. Other public sector infrastructure bodies need to play a similar role and can learn from the work that has been done with local authorities. National government will have an important role to play in Scotland and Wales and, particularly through Together We Can and Capacity Builders, can play a supportive role in England, too.

Bibliography

This bibliography contains documents referred to in the text and other key policy documents in England, Scotland and Wales.

National policy documents

England

DCLG (Department for Communities and Local Government) (2006a) *Strong and prosperous communities: The local government White Paper*, Cm 6939, London: DCLG.

DCLG (Department for Communities and Local Government) (2006b) *The Community Development Challenge*, London: DCLG.

SEU (Social Exclusion Unit) (2001) *A new commitment to neighbourhood renewal: A national strategy action plan*, London: Cabinet Office.

Scotland

Carley, M. (2004) *Implementing community planning: Building for the future of local governance*, Edinburgh: Communities Scotland.

Scottish Executive (2006) *People and place: Regeneration policy statement*, Edinburgh: Scottish Executive.

Wales

Anti-Poverty Network Cymru (2006) *Walking the talk: Communities on Communities First* (available from http://oxfamgb.org/ukpp/).

Welsh Assembly Government (2006a) *Interim evaluation of Communities First*, Cardiff: Welsh Assembly Government.

Welsh Assembly Government (2006b) *Beyond boundaries: Citizen-centred local services for Wales* ('the Beecham review'), Cardiff: Welsh Assembly Government.

Welsh Assembly Government (2006c) *National Housing Strategy for Wales: A selective review*, Cardiff: Welsh Assembly Government.

Welsh Assembly Government (2006) *Making the connections: Delivering beyond boundaries*, Cardiff: Welsh Assembly Government.

Local authority documents

IDeA (Improvement and Development Agency) (2006) *Making it real: A report of the pilot partnership improvement programme with voluntary and community organisations and local authorities*, London: IDeA (www.idea.gov.uk).

LGA (Local Government Association) (2005) *Closer to people: A new vision for local government*, London: LGA.

Report text references

Adamson, D. (2006) 'Community regeneration policy, the state and civil society', in G. Day, D. Dunkerley and A. Thompson (eds) *Civil society in Wales: Policy, politics and people*, Cardiff: University of Wales Press.

Edwards, A., Barnes, M., Plewis, I., Morris, K. et al (2006) *Working to prevent the social exclusion of children and young people: Final lessons from the national evaluation of the Children's Fund*, DfES Research Report 734, London: DfES.

HACT (Housing Associations Charitable Trust) (2006) *An opportunity waiting to happen*, London: HACT.

Hilder, P. (2005) *Seeing the wood for the trees: The evolving landscape for neighbourhood arrangements*, London: The Young Foundation and Transforming Neighbourhoods Programme.

ODPM (Office of the Deputy Prime Minister) (2005) *Making connections: An evaluation of the Community Participation Programmes*, London: ODPM.

Appendix 1: Profile of the neighbourhood organisations involved in the Programme

England

South West

Boscombe Working Community Partnership, Bournemouth

Boscombe was once one of the most prosperous areas of Bournemouth. With the decline in the tourist trade the area has declined. The neighbourhood now qualifies on every indicator in the statistics of poverty and crime, including substantial substance abuse; drug dealing; and prostitution.

The Boscombe Working Community Partnership was set up in 2001 as part of the Single Regeneration Budget 6 (SRB6) funding programme, following a successful SRB4 programme. Residents of Boscombe hold slightly more than half the seats on the board, which acts as the main body responsible for approving SRB-funded projects. The many valuable projects supported by the Partnership include: the Boscombe Arts Festival, the establishment of a credit union, youth work, community training grants, college outreach provision, an employment and skills programme for those in recovery, new business grants, a family support programme, environmental and architectural improvements and many others.

Broad Street Community Council, Swindon

The Broad Street area lies close to Swindon town centre, with 45% black and minority ethnic (BME) residents. At the start of the Programme there was felt to be a language barrier and separation between the different ethnic communities in the area. Local problems included drug dealing; street prostitution; and poor maintenance and street cleaning.

The Community Council is a resident-led voluntary organisation established in the 1970s to improve the quality of life for local residents. In spite of a lack of funding when the Neighbourhood Programme began, members of the Community Council had already tackled street prostitution and kerb crawling and set up a Street Watch in partnership with the police. When joining the Neighbourhood Programme, a separate 'JRF Group' was set up to secure better links with, and stronger involvement from, the various minority ethnic groups in the area.

Over time this group coalesced into an effective multi-ethnic network for the neighbourhood and in August 2006 the JRF Group was relaunched as Broadgreen Organisation for Neighbourhood Development.

St Pauls Unlimited Community Partnership, Bristol

St Pauls is a highly deprived inner-city neighbourhood in Bristol and is the most diverse neighbourhood in the city. The population of approximately 6,000 people includes both a stable multicultural community and a transient community accessing social housing and hostels.

St Pauls Unlimited Community Partnership is a resident-led partnership set up in 2002 to develop a plan for the area, supported by Neighbourhood Renewal funding. The Partnership includes representation from a number of public agencies including the police and the city council housing, planning and economic development departments. Grassroots community representation has been built into its structure, with BME groups and local areas within the neighbourhood all represented, and community consultation is a core function. The council has worked through St Pauls Unlimited to find ways of reaching and talking to people who do not normally get involved in community activities.

Tamar Development Trust, Plymouth

Barne Barton is a former Ministry of Defence (MoD) estate in the St Budeaux area of Plymouth. As the MoD scaled down activities, homes on the estate were sold to housing associations. The community, of approximately 5,000 people, has experience high unemployment levels, large numbers of single parents and low-income levels, coupled with a lack of shops and other facilities.

Barne Barton Community Action Group was established in 1995, initially prompted by the lack of basic services in the community following the withdrawal of naval facilities. In 2000 the group became the Barne Barton Community Action Trust in order both to raise its profile and to access funding. In 2003 the Trust changed its name to the Tamar Development Trust Ltd. The organisation secured SRB funding followed by Neighbourhood Renewal funding to develop a range of neighbourhood-led activities and services. These have included training programmes and a community safety wardens scheme. The organisation is also the accountable body for a Surestart scheme.

In 2006 the Trust went into receivership and the trustees were not prepared to take the risk of continuing to trade.

West Midlands

Canley Residents Action Group

Canley is a peripheral estate of Coventry with a population of nearly 5,000. Because it is situated within a more affluent ward of the city the neighbourhood suffers from a dilution of its statistics of deprivation, which therefore excludes it from much regeneration funding. There are few community or voluntary organisations in the area and some local shops have gone out of business following the development of an out-of-town shopping centre.

Canley Residents Action Group is based in the centre of the estate. As the JRF involvement drew to a close, a major regeneration programme was announced for the area. This represents a massive investment that aims to make Canley more prosperous, with improved road links, a new local school and selective redevelopment aimed at developing a more mixed community. The hope was that this would be an opportunity for the Group to increase its membership and widen the area it claimed to cover in order to have more influence. However, this has not been the case. The Canley Regeneration Project Board has therefore agreed to a proposal from Coventry Council to promote a new Canley Forum. The Group has now been dissolved and its members will choose whether to take part in the new Forum.

Castle Vale Housing Action Trust, Birmingham

Castle Vale is Birmingham's largest post-war housing estate, situated seven miles north east of the city centre. Built between 1964 and 1969 to house families displaced by the slum clearance programme, Castle Vale quickly began to experience problems of an economic and social nature, as well as physical problems due to the use of untested construction techniques.

Castle Vale Housing Action Trust was established in 1993 to undertake a major reconstruction of the estate over a 10-year period. The Trust set a vision of working with residents and others to create a self-sustaining community living in high-quality homes in a pleasant and safe environment. It has developed into one of the biggest community regeneration schemes of its kind in Britain. When the Trust joined the JRF Programme it was approaching the winding up of the Housing Action Trust in 2005 and exploring options for a successor body to sustain developments. Castle Vale Community Housing Association now leads community activity in Castle Vale and a Community Neighbourhood Partnership Board has now been developed bringing together the Association and other partners.

Lodge Farm Community Network, Dudley

Lodge Farm is a small housing estate (218 residences) within the Metropolitan Borough of Dudley, built in the Second World War by German and Italian prisoners of war. The estate is geographically isolated, surrounded by a nature reserve with a nearby reservoir. The estate has a community centre (housed in rather dilapidated units built in 1979 as a temporary measure), a shop and a small Baptist church. Most services, such as the housing office, social services and libraries, are based in nearby Netherton. A concern of many local residents has been that they feel the estate is a forgotten area.

Although community activities for younger residents had been organised for many years, the Lodge Farm Community Network was only formally established in about 2001. Over the past two years, the Community Network has developed stronger links with the Netherton Children's Centre, Black Country Housing and Community Services Ltd and other service agencies. Currently, the Wolverhampton Wanderers Community Team is running dusk-to-midnight football coaching on the estate and the neighbouring area, attracting around 90 youngsters to each session.

The progress that has been made has encouraged the residents and their supporting service agencies to pursue an ambitious long-term aim of replacing its inadequate 'portakabin' community facilities with a permanent building.

Malvern

Pickersleigh is a large social housing estate with a population of approximately 6,000 in the affluent market town of Malvern. Local issues include: relatively high levels of unemployment, crime and anti-social behaviour; the initial lack of a comprehensive regeneration strategy for the area; the need to strengthen participation by local residents in local projects and decision-making; and improving access to a local community centre. A positive vote for stock transfer led to the estate becoming the responsibility of Elgar Housing Association.

A community development worker was appointed in 2002. Involvement in the JRF Programme initially focused on supporting the development of the Oak Crescent Residents Group with the intent of rolling out the methods of developing the group to other streets. But it proved impossible to sustain a group covering such a small number of residences and the Group folded.

The Pickersleigh Regeneration Strategy Working Group was then established to develop an action plan for the whole ward. The group consists of local residents, professionals, councillors and local authority officers. Lessons learnt led to the community development worker developing a different approach through less formal, 'front-room' meetings, which have been held to increase participation, identify the real local issues and recruit residents to sit on the Pickersleigh Strategy Group.

These methods of engaging with residents are proving successful, and an Operational and Strategic Plan has now been drawn up through the cooperation of residents, the police, the housing association, the school and the environmental group with some support from the district council.

Yorkshire and Humber

Boothtown Community Partnership, Halifax

Boothtown is a neighbourhood on the north-east side of Halifax with a population of approximately 6,000. It is an area of mixed owner-occupier and rented housing adjacent to Halifax town centre. At the start of the Programme, local facilities were poor compared to other neighbourhoods of a similar size, with no youth or community centres, and the area suffered from a drugs problem with an upsurge in house burglaries.

The Boothtown Community Partnership was established in 2002 to improve the quality of life in a part of Halifax where many people felt neglected by the council and regeneration-type programmes. A steering committee consisting of about 12 local people was established and secured a new facility for the neighbourhood, a small centre incorporating changing rooms on the sports field alongside the local primary school.

The partnership is now a well-established part of the community sector scene in Calderdale offering a range of activities at the centre. It has also developed an active youth forum and organises a very successful annual food and dance festival.

Eastfield Neighbourhood Partnership (Eastfield Pact)

Eastfield is a suburb of Scarborough built in the 1940s and 1950s, approximately three miles from the town centre. The Eastfield ward is an area of predominantly local authority housing with a population of just over 3,000. The ward ranks within the top 10% most deprived wards in the Index of Multiple Deprivation.

Eastfield Pact was established in April 2001 as one of seven new neighbourhood organisations initiated by Scarborough Council to help administer European funding under the Objective 2 programme (2000-06). The Partnership, when joining the programme, involved seven residents in a board of 36 members. A key objective has been developing a more community-led partnership.

Key achievements in working towards this objective have included: the establishment of the neighbourhood partnership as a charitable company (as the successor body to Eastfield Pact); the establishment of the Eastfield Residents Group; resident involvement in the development of Neighbourhood Management arrangements; involvement in strategic development of a nearby business park to ensure economic opportunities for local people; and the revival of the Eastfield Carnival.

Integrate, Todmorden

Todmorden, in Calderdale, is a town of approximately 10,000 people of whom approximately 300 people are Asian. Most of the Asian population lives within half a mile of the town centre. Traditional employment is based in the declining textile industry and unemployment is well above the national average.

Integrate is a newly established Asian community organisation in the town. It grew out of a small group who secured some initial funding to organise football for young people from the local mosque. The initiator of this group had a much wider vision about the need to help the small local Asian community overcome its isolation and play a much more active role in the life of the town. He also felt strongly that the town of Todmorden itself needed to be more 'integrated' into the wider local authority area of Calderdale as Todmorden was often forgotten by the power holders in Halifax. Integrate still organises sporting activities for young people but has raised its profile within Todmorden and developed good links with Todmorden Together (SRB5) and with Adult and Community Learning.

Norfolk Park Community Forum, Sheffield

Norfolk Park is an inner-city estate in Sheffield initially developed as a council estate with nearly 3,000 properties in the 1960s. Over recent years the area has been subject to a major housing regeneration programme. The area has been a victim of the classic cycle of urban decline. Extended and slow progress on demolition and new build in the area has 'magnified' the cycle of decline.

The Norfolk Park Community Forum was established in the mid-1990s to take the lead in ensuring that the views of the local community were taken into account in the regeneration programme. It grew steadily, and by 2004 had developed a number of initiatives designed to respond to local needs, including the one-stop advice centre, childcare, basic skills training and an older people's support project. The Forum established a new community company, Parklands Community Ventures, alongside its continued role in seeking to influence regeneration plans. In autumn 2006 financial difficulties forced Parklands Community Ventures out of business and as result the Forum went into liquidation. Some activities established by the Forum are continuing but at the time of going to print the plans of local people to develop a future organisation are still uncertain.

Scotland

Empowering Community Group, Levern Valley, East Renfrewshire

Levern Valley (population approximately 20,000) includes the town of Barrhead and the villages of Neilston and Uplawmoor. Local issues include community safety; drug and alcohol misuse; and lack of community premises.

The Empowering Community Group was established in 2001 to allocate Empowering Communities funding received by Levern Valley Partnership from the Scottish Executive. Members of the group are also community representatives on the Levern Valley Partnership Board. Funding was to be used for training and other activities that help to involve people in local democracy and has included support to local organisations such as a youth initiative, a disabled forum and a tenants' and residents' association, and other initiatives including visits to the Scottish Parliament and the provision of computers for community representatives. With the demise of Empowering Communities funding, the future of the Group is uncertain. It is exploring the possibility of expanding its membership and boundaries to provide a similar function in administering the Community Voices funding programme across the East Renfrewshire Community Planning area.

Pilton Partnership, Edinburgh

Greater Pilton (population approximately 25,000) lies to the north of Edinburgh city centre. It comprises five distinct neighbourhoods built between the 1950s and 1960s. Socially rented housing accounts for around 50% of all housing. The area is characterised by the highest levels of deprivation in Lothian. The underlying issue of material poverty impacts on a range of other issues including health.

The Pilton Partnership was formed in 1990 around a successful bid for funding through the Third European Anti-poverty Programme. The current Partnership is one between local councillors and community representatives selected from their local communities. The Partnership has a core team including three full-time and two part-time development workers funded through the City of Edinburgh Council Corporate Services.

Since 1994 the Partnership has had three main areas of responsibility:

- to encourage and support community participation and community involvement in the regeneration process;
- the management of the community's SIP, formerly known as Urban Aid. This SIP encompasses Pilton's five neighbourhoods;
- the development of projects and services that help to address poverty and the maximisation of community resources.

The Partnership has carried out a series of community consultation exercises to involve local people in reviewing existing community structures and the lessons learnt in order to develop effective structures for the future, and seeks to influence the development of new community planning structures and arrangements in the area.

Skypoint/Faifley Neighbourhood Forum, Clydebank

Faifley is an estate in Clydebank with a population of approximately 4,300. Skypoint Faifley was a locally initiated development trust, involved in regenerating a local primary school as a base for community activities and enterprises including an arts programme, market garden and community cafe, training initiatives and youth services.

However, shortly after the Programme began this organisation was declared insolvent on the instigation of its main creditor, the local authority. Following a period of review a new agreement was reached for Faifley Neighbourhood Forum to become part of the Programme.

The Neighbourhood Forum is a broad-based organisation for all residents of Faifley. It has been meeting monthly for four years to discuss local issues, such as traffic management, public safety and the needs of young people. Meetings also involve local councillors, representatives from the local housing association and the police. The Forum has developed close links with local youth programmes and is subsequently developing its own sub-committee for young people. It has also supported the construction of new sculptures acting as an entrance and enhanced identity for the neighbourhood. The Forum is involved, as a user, in the management of Skypoint, which continues to be a vital community resource. As a result of its involvement in the JRF Programme, the Forum has now produced a Community Plan for Faifley to be published in early 2007.

Southside Housing Association, East Pollokshields, Glasgow

East Pollokshields is a multi-racial, inner-city area of Glasgow, home to the largest minority ethnic population in Scotland. The majority population in the tenement properties in the area are from an Asian, mainly Pakistani, background.

During 2003 Southside Housing Association, most of whose stock is in East Pollokshields, decided that more effort was needed to address underlying issues of deprivation and racial exclusion facing the neighbourhood. The Association is a fairly small community-based association that wanted to take a more strategic neighbourhood approach and at the beginning of the JRF Programme had just appointed a community development officer.

A key subsequent area of development has been the bringing together of the many community organisations active in the neighbourhood into one new formal partnership – the Pollokshields East Partnership. This partnership has been instrumental in steering a community consultation process that resulted in the East Pollokshields Community Plan. In order to be more effective in both attracting funding and driving forward the implementation of an action plan, the partnership is now developing into a Community Development Trust.

Wales

Caia Park Partnership, Wrexham

Caia Park in Wrexham is the largest estate in North Wales, with a population of 14,000. There used to be few facilities for residents on the estate and local problems included: low income; high unemployment; low skills; car crime; and drugs. The area comprises two Communities First wards: Caia and Queensway.

Caia Park Partnership was formed in 1995 by local community activists and established as a community development organisation and registered charity. The partnership is now well established, owning several buildings and providing a range of services (children and young people; tenancy support and family services; volunteering and training; a Healthy

Living Centre; and, recently, English language and bilingual advice to recent migrants from Poland and other Eastern European countries).

Gellideg Foundation Group, Merthyr Tydfil

Gellideg, a mile outside Merthyr Tydfil, is a local authority estate of 628 dwellings built in the 1940s. The estate has a high percentage of young people, many of whom experience low educational achievement and are disadvantaged by the poor local physical environment. Other local issues include: a high level of crime and fear of crime; rundown housing stock; poor quality services; and the neglected physical aspect of the estate.

The Gellideg Foundation Group grew from six mothers attending a parental 'accelerated learning' group, in 1999. This led them to organise monthly discos in the church hall. Funding was acquired in 2001. They moved on to doing their own consultation, renovating the church hall and developing an all-weather play space as the young boys asked for football. They have turned one block of derelict flats into a Healthy Living Centre and are starting to use the renovation of the next block as a training programme in building and basic education skills and as access to college. The Group has grown from a small to a medium-sized organisation employing 22 staff.

Llanharan Community Development Project, Rhondda Cynon Taff

The three mining villages of Llanharan, Brynna and Bryncae in the Rhondda have a combined population of approx 8,000. The area includes council housing with serious social and economic deprivation among more affluent owner-occupied housing.

The Llanharan Community Development Project was established in the mid-1990s. The project has a board with resident majority and a strong focus on: young people; training; advice work; and lifelong learning. The project obtained National Lottery funding to renovate an old billiard hall as a drop-in centre for young people, which was opened in 1998. In 2000 further funding was secured to develop an adjacent house for additional activities, and subsequently the project has started to provide youth work through Service Level Agreements with the local authority.

Ty Sign Local Communities Partnership, Newport

Ty Sign is an isolated community located on a steep hill near Risca in Caerphilly, South Wales, and is one of Gwent's largest estates (population approximately 5,200). Problems include families with social problems; high levels of crime and disorder; the only single occupancy flats in the county; and deprivation that is hidden by the more affluent surrounding areas. The area suffers from a serious lack of community facilities (for youth, for health and meeting places).

The Ty Sign Local Communities Partnership was brand new at the start of the Programme and has opened a resource centre for youth activities and community events. It works with the local council and a supportive partnership group, with the long-term hope of establishing a community centre. The partnership is open to everyone living or working in the area and is managed by a committee of local residents, councillors and representatives of community and voluntary groups.

Appendix 2: Neighbourhood Programme joint projects: summary of key messages

As part of the Neighbourhood Programme, four 'joint projects' were commissioned on key cross-cutting themes that were identified as important by several of the neighbourhoods. The work was carried out by facilitators who worked through a variety of methods including: surveys; workshops; visits to the neighbourhoods; and collecting information from other agencies.

The main lessons from each of these projects are outlined in four summaries – 'Community engagement and community leadership', 'Funding', 'Diversity' and 'Being taken seriously by power holders' – available as free downloads from the Joseph Rowntree Foundation website: www.jrf.org.uk

Appendix 3: Bringing 'Neighbourhood' Centre Stage events

As part of the Neighbourhood Programme three events under the banner of Bringing 'Neighbourhood' Centre Stage were held for local authorities and their partners to explore the role for neighbourhoods in local governance and the links between neighbourhood regeneration and service delivery. They were targeted at council chief executives, leaders and other senior officers, and all were attended by Lord Best together with other JRF directors and staff and one or two practitioners from the Neighbourhood Programme. The events included:

1. A 24-hour event hosted jointly with the Neighbourhood Renewal Unit in Liverpool and attended by seven unitary authorities. Discussions at this event explored the neighbourhood agenda in the context of the National Strategy for Neighbourhood Renewal and in particular the development of neighbourhood management. A concluding summary of the seminar identified the following key points as emerging from discussions:
   - the need for any programme to bring neighbourhoods centre stage to have cross-party consensus locally and nationally;
   - the need for local authorities bsoth to 'let go' and to take control of the change process required;
   - engagement at neighbourhood level will offer the possibility of a new role for backbench councillors requiring new skills;
   - devolving services through neighbourhood management should be a first priority with changes to local governance structures following as needed;
   - the shift to service delivery and accompanying governance arrangements should not be confined to deprived neighbourhoods but rolled out city-wide so that benefits have real political visibility and durability.

2. A 24-hour event hosted jointly with Communities Scotland in Edinburgh and attended by representatives of 10 local authorities, partner agencies including the police, the NHS and community organisations and the Scottish Executive. This provided an opportunity to explore progress and challenges in relation to the development of Community Planning Partnerships (CPPs). As part of this discussion one of the neighbourhood-based organisations from the Neighbourhood Programme made a presentation challenging the extent to which a number of agencies involved in community planning were committed to community engagement. At the end of the event four key themes were suggested for future consideration:
   - ways of linking, through locality plans, the area level at which service providers often want to organise to the neighbourhood level that is most appropriate for nurturing genuine local participation;
   - how to foster innovation within local authorities in changing organisational cultures to value community empowerment and partnership working;
   - the need to rethink the roles and relationships of key players in community planning including officers, councillors, community activists and other stakeholders;

- the need for a cross-party approach, locally and in the Scottish Parliament to ensure there is a steady, long-term process of learning and improvement.

3. A one-day event hosted jointly with the Welsh Assembly Government and attended by representatives of 10 county and county borough councils, the Wales Council for Voluntary Action and community organisations. This provided an opportunity to explore the neighbourhood agenda in the context of evolving Welsh Assembly Government strategies and policies, including the Communities First programme and the Beecham report (Welsh Assembly Government, 2006a), which had been published just two days before the event. A number of 'common threads' ran through the day's presentations and workshops including:

   - the 'implementation gaps' revealed not only by the JRF Neighbourhood Programme and research but also by the challenges and barriers faced by the Communities First Programme and other forms of community engagement;
   - the positive lessons from experience from the Neighbourhood Programme and other good practice in Wales;
   - the challenge of acting on the Beecham report proposals;
   - new roles for councillors and community and town councils.

These events – as well as a series of meetings with civil servants in all three countries – were an opportunity to promote discussion between senior local authority personnel and gain commitment to a neighbourhood approach.

Appendix 4: Neighbourhood Programme personnel

Programme manager

John Low

Facilitators

England

Jenny Lynn (Yorkshire and Humber)

Trish McCue (South West)

Chris Wadhams (West Midlands)

Wales

Mel Witherden

Scotland

Michael Carley

Advisory group

The following members served on the advisory group for all or part of the Programme

Dave Adamson, University of Glamorgan

Shafiq Ahmed, Bradford City Council

Andrew Barnett, Joseph Rowntree Foundation

Richard Crossley, Department for Communities and Local Government

Alison Gilchrist, Community Development Foundation

Alison Hill, Caia Park Partnership Ltd

Joan Hubbard, Norfolk Park Community Forum

Richard Kemp, Chair. JRF Neighbourhood Programme Advisory Group

Jerry le Sueur, Independent Consultant

Angus McCabe, Advisor to the Evaluation Team

Theresa McDonagh, Joseph Rowntree Foundation

Sean McGonigle, New Deal for Communities Team

Steven Nesbit, Government Office for Yorkshire and The Humber

Jacky Preston, Community Advisor

Tony Stoller, Joseph Rowntree Foundation Trustee

Archie Thomson, Renton Community Development Trust

Appendix 5:
Glossary: relevant policies and programmes

England

Local Area Agreements (LAAs): three-year agreements between government, the local authority and its major delivery partners in an area (working through LSPs), which set out the agreed priorities and targets for the area. They are based on Sustainable Communities Strategies, likewise agreed between partners, which set out the broader vision and priorities for the area.

Local Strategic Partnership (LSP): a non-statutory, multi-agency body, which matches local authority boundaries, and aims to bring together at a local level the different parts of the public, private, community and voluntary sectors.

National Community Forum: a small group of experienced residents and paid workers from neighbourhood level formed to advise government on Neighbourhood Renewal policy.

National Strategy for Neighbourhood Renewal: a '10-to-20-year plan to turn round poor neighbourhoods, to reduce dependency and to empower local communities' in order that 'no one' should be 'seriously disadvantaged by where they live'.

Neighbourhood Management Pathfinders (NMPs): a seven-year programme in 35 localities across England designed to lever change in mainstream services.

Neighbourhood Renewal Fund (NRF): funding channelled through Local Strategic Partnerships (LSPs) in 88 priority local authority areas of England to support their Local Neighbourhood Renewal Strategies.

Neighbourhood Wardens: a three-year pilot programme in 84 neighbourhoods across England.

New Deal for Communities (NDC): a 10-year project-based programme in England, investing significant funds in 39 localities.

Single Community Programme: provided infrastructure support in the 88 priority areas to local groups and a route to influence the LSP through a Community Empowerment Network in each locality.

Single Regeneration Budget (SRB): The SRB programme aimed to enhance the employment prospects, education and skills of local people and to tackle the needs of communities in the most deprived areas.

Sustainable Community Plan: launched in England in 2003. The Plan sets out a long-term programme of action for delivering sustainable communities in both urban and rural areas. It aims to tackle housing supply issues in the South East and low demand in other parts of the country, to bring all social housing up to the Decent Homes Standard by 2010, to protect the countryside and to improve the quality of public spaces.

Scotland

Better Neighbourhood Services Fund: covered the period 2001-05 and introduced in 12 pathfinder areas to improve services for people living in disadvantaged areas.

Community Empowerment Fund: designed to strengthen community participation in SIPs. These included Community Empowerment Funds to support community engagement.

Community Planning: a statutory framework of duties for institutional stakeholders to engage with citizens in developing a Community Plan to improve the delivery of services and meet the aspirations of communities.

Community Regeneration Fund: a £318 million fund introduced in 2004, targeted at the 15% most disadvantaged neighbourhoods in Scotland.

Community Voices Programme: a three-year funding programme introduced in 2005 to support Community Planning Partnerships to deliver community engagement.

Social Inclusion Partnerships (SIPs): Successor to WfC established in 2002. There were 48 SIPs, of which 34 were area-based and 14 thematic.

Working for Communities (WfC) Partnership pathfinders: set up in 1998 to test innovative local service delivery and budgeting in 13 disadvantaged neighbourhoods.

Wales

Communities First Programme (Wales): a 10-year programme through which special funds are disbursed to 132 neighbourhoods and 10 communities of interest.

Objective 1 programmes: Objective 1 targets European Union Structural Funds on areas that have an economy falling well behind the European average for wealth creation.

Resource sheet A: Community Empowerment framework

This framework was developed by the evaluation team to reflect the range of community empowerment issues being faced by projects in the JRF Neighbourhood Programme. It was produced as a resource for organisations when they were considering action plans.

Problem	What would make change happen? (Rationale for the project)	How do you plan to make change happen? (Aims and objectives)	What results do you want to see? (Outcomes of the project)
Analysis			
No one has analysed local problems and assets Lack of direction – activity tends to be reactive rather than proactive	Consultation is needed with local communities to identify their needs and plan action	Profile community needs and assets Draw up an action plan with short- and medium-term objectives to guide your work	A plan of action that local communities feel a part of
Engagement			
People are not engaged, little activity is going on locally to tackle problems	Community development is needed to encourage people to engage with the project	Set up community development and outreach projects Develop a strategy to communicate with people and tell them what your project is all about	Local communities are engaged in a variety of activities and tackling local problems

Problem	What would make change happen? (Rationale for the project)	How you plan to make change happen? (Aims and objectives)	What results do you want to see? (Outcomes of the project)
Capacity Lack of leadership; lack of organisational ability; low level of skills; low level of resources	Sustainable leadership and organisational ability are needed to plan and coordinate action and raise funds	Provide opportunities to develop: • leaders and organisations • management skills • team building and accountability • fundraising skills	Effective and sustainable organisations and accountable leadership Sustainable funding and assets
Cohesion The community is divided and fragmented	Common ground, mutual respect and understanding between communities and individuals	Develop negotiating, mediation and conflict resolution skills Hold events and meetings to bring different groups together	Local communities acting effectively together
Power and influence Those who have power ignore the needs of the community; policy is not geared to local need and the community is not involved in decision making	People in power need a greater understanding of the needs of the community and the skills to communicate effectively with local people Confidence and community-owned assets, rather than local authority-owned assets, can give the community greater power	Develop political, promotional and negotiating skills Develop greater understanding and rapport with statutory bodies and other partners Capacity building with statutory bodies and other partners so that they engage more effectively with communities Develop the skills and resources to build up community-owned assets and services	Be taken seriously by power holders; work more effectively with them; make changes in policy and practice Effective management of community assets and services

Resource sheet B:
Making changes: a recording table

This is a blank, expanded version of resource sheet A. It provides a structure and recording table for organisations when considering key issues and problems and how to address them.

Problems *What problems are you trying to address?*	What would make change happen? *(Rationale)*	How do you plan to make change happen? *(Aims and objectives)*	What results do you want to see? *(Outcomes)*	What could you use to measure progress? *(Indicators)*

Resource sheet C:
Evaluation planning: a recording table

This table can be used by organisations when developing an evaluation action plan. For each measure of progress (indicator) it will be important to identify what information is gathered through existing procedures, what additional information will need to be gathered, and how, by whom and by when.

Indicators	What information do you already have?	What additional information will you need?	What methods will you use to gather the additional information?	Who will take responsibility for gathering this information?	How long will they have?

Resource sheet D: Processes for reviewing progress against action plans

This is a summary of the kinds of processes used by some of the neighbourhood organisations in the JRF Programme when reviewing their action plans.

Task	Process
Context Identify the context in which the project is operating and particularly any changes (positive and negative) since action plan was first developed, eg more sympathetic local political climate, funding having been cut/ new funding opportunities, etc	Use flipchart to log both key contextual factors when action plan first developed and key changes in context. Different colours or symbols may be used for positive contextual factors (opportunities) and negative ones (threats)
Aims and objectives Identify extent to which aims and objectives have been achieved	Use large copies of action plan aims and objectives on wall. Identify how far met by traffic light colours (green/amber/red) sticky dots or marker pens. Individual participants to place marks Together consider and discuss marks and use a 1–5 grading (1= not met at all, 5 = fully met) to assess progress for each aim and mark onto action plan
What has worked well? What have been the difficulties?	Discussion – record onto flipchart
What should we keep? What should we drop? What do we want to add?	Use information and views recorded in preceding steps to consider answers to these questions
Complete revised action plan with timescales etc	Use a proforma for recording this

Resource sheet E: Community 'snakes and ladders': to identify organisational turning points

This exercise was used at one of the Neighbourhood Programme networking events as a way for organisations to share and log some of the key factors that either progressed or hampered the development of their organisation.

Process	Resources
1. Participants, working with others from the same organisation, write on post-it notes key development turning points for their own organisations over last 4 years. These should be limited to 8 turning points.	Prompt cards in middle of table Post-it notes (if more than one group, use different colours for each)
2. Each participant presents his/her turning points and puts them on the flipchart. Working together, participants cluster similar cards (turning points) on a separate flipchart. 3. For each cluster there is a very brief discussion about how these turning points have helped and/or hampered progress. Those that have helped are put into left-hand 'ladder' column and those that have hampered into the right-hand 'snakes' column.	Flipchart with 2 columns. Left column titled 'ladders' and right titled 'snakes'
4. Make up snakes and ladders game – stick post-its onto boxes and stick on snakes and ladders.	Outline grid plus snakes and ladders symbols Blu-tak
5. Play the game! If there is more than one group they could then swap games and play each others.	Prepared snakes and ladders game plus dice

Examples of prompt cards

Moved into our own
community building

Development worker
resigned

Single Regeneration
Budget funding ended

Community Planning
Partnership set up

Open day in May 2004
attracted three new
committee members

The chair finally left!

Went to Communities
First conference – got
lots of new ideas

Held away day to
review our action plan
and developed clearer
way forward

Neighbourhood snakes and ladders

Example from the Neighbourhood Programme

48	47 Funding application fails leading to cutbacks in activities	46	45	44 Leading volunteer dies and sets us all back	43	42	41 Council axes community safety development
33	34	35 Moved into our own community building	36	37 Change of chair	38 Individuals who block, hold group to ransom	39	40
32	31 Problems with contractors	30	29	28	27	26	25
17	18 Setting up Community Planning Partnership – left group powerless	19	20	21	22 Sack the community development worker	23 Young people get involved in community forum	24
16	15	14 Lack of respect for community reps from councillors	13	12 Changes in committee – jolted out of complacency, fresh ideas and new motivation	11	10	9 Funding secured for training and equipment
1 Local resident appointed as worker – contacts make the community festival a success	2	3	4 Successful food and dance festival	5	6 Front-room meetings – increase involvement in residents' association	7	8

Resource sheet F: Neighbourhood Protocol: an example

The Caia Park Partnership worked with other local community agencies to develop the following Neighbourhood Protocol agreement.

Mission statement and guidelines for the partnership of community agencies working in Caia Park, Wrexham

The partners

The following organisations are committed to pursuing the aims of this agreement:

- Caia Park Communities First
- Caia Park Partnership
- The Venture
- Caia Park Community Council (informally, not as a full signatory).

The mission

The partner organisations will work together with the aims of:

- making the most effective use of the resources available to Caia Park;
- ensuring that services delivered locally are of the highest possible standard and relevant to the needs of residents;
- making the work of local agencies more understandable, accessible and accountable to local residents;
- increasing joint working between the partner agencies;
- continuing to improve the profile of Caia Park, and the understanding of its needs among individuals and organisations outside the community.

Guidelines for the work of the agencies

The principles

The partner organisations will work together to achieve this mission by:

1. Ensuring that their managers, staff, volunteers, trustees/directors and members are aware of the purpose and contents of this agreement.
2. Sharing information with one another on their current and future work for the Caia Park community to enable the partners to work together effectively.
3. Encouraging all staff within each organisation to engage in good communication with colleagues from other agencies and with members of the community.

4. Discouraging rumour and uninformed criticisms about partner organisations, and instead raising any difficulties through the proper channels so that they can be dealt with quickly and efficiently by the appropriate officers.
5. Respecting the particular responsibilities and expertise of other partners.
6. Planning the use of resources more effectively to avoid duplication, and actively seeking opportunities for consultation and joint work with partners.
7. Continuing to develop structures that enhance and strengthen cooperation.
8. Developing best practice to promote active community involvement.
9. Where appropriate, working collaboratively with other voluntary and public sector agencies and funders.

The practical arrangements

The principles set out above will be achieved through the following practical arrangements. The list is not intended to be comprehensive, and partners will aim to develop other suitable approaches in due course.

1. *Chief officers' meetings:* there will be regular meetings between the chief officers of the partner organisations:
   - The purpose of these meetings is to exchange information about current and future activities and plans, to discuss matters of common interest in the work that they carry out, and to share and explore issues of concern between the partners.
   - The meetings will be held at least once every month.
   - If a chief officer is not able to attend, they must arrange for a well-briefed deputy to attend in their place who can speak for the organisation and effectively communicate back the outcomes of the meeting.
   - It is the chief officers' responsibility to ensure that the practical arrangements below are implemented.

2. *Communications:* each chief officer takes responsibility for ensuring there are well-developed two-way communications within their organisation so that other managers and staff can easily pass on information that is relevant to partners, and so that information from partners can penetrate to all levels of their organisation. Also, formal and informal opportunities will be actively created for staff from different organisations to come together to discuss issues of common interest. These arrangements will be reviewed from time to time to make sure they are working.

3. *Joint community consultations:* the partner organisations will collaborate on organising and publicising at least one community consultation event each year, in response to key local priorities. They will explore other opportunities for joint consultations.

4. *Joint publications:* the partners will:
   - prepare and publish a highly readable Caia Park Review each year that celebrates the work of all partner agencies and their other partners on behalf of Caia Park, and will circulate it widely in the community;
   - seek opportunities for other joint publications, such as newsletters and bulletins.

5. *Structures for collaboration and joint strategy making:* the partners will work together to explore the possibility of jointly establishing a structure whose functions might include:
   - enhancing the accountability of partner agencies to the Caia Park community;
   - developing best practice to promote active community involvement;
   - fostering joint working between the partners and with other agencies;

- strategic planning for Caia Park on key local issues;
- addressing long-term funding and sustainability issues;
- spearheading Neighbourhood Management for Caia Park.

6. *Continuing collaboration:* the present agreement is a start. Partners will review progress, and periodically develop other mechanisms for joint working.

7. *The Wrexham Compact:* the partners will work together with Wrexham County Borough Council to achieve the successful implementation in Caia Park of the Wrexham Compact between the council and the voluntary sector.

We agree to abide by the terms of this agreement:

Chair, Caia Park Communities First

Date

Chair, Caia Park Partnership

Date

Chair, The Venture

Date